ACCORDING TO WARREN BUFFETT

Kimon Sarandos Aylett

BuffettBoy

Scan the QR Code or copy the link to access the world of BuffettBoy

linktr.ee/buffettboy

"People can relate to Warren with his Midwestern attitudes and values, his character, his reputation and the fact that he speaks the truth. No other CEO has quite the draw that Warren Buffett has."
- Robert Miles, author of the *Warren Buffett CEO*

"What struck me at the meeting was the incredible clarity of their thinking. It is so simple and so rational, an uncomplicated type of thinking" - Laurie Dippenaar, Ex-Chairman and Co-Founder of FirstRand, Africa's largest listed financial services group (by market capitalization). Six-time Berkshire Hathaway attendee.

"*After discovering Mr. Buffett and Mr. Munger, Warren and Charlie as the world knows them, it completely changed my mind about so many things*"- Alec Hogg, Financial journalist, founder of BizNews.com, and author of *How To Invest Like Warren Buffett: Discover the Wisdom of the World's Greatest Wealth Creator*. Nine-time Berkshire Hathaway attendee.

"*Your dad has a term, 'We go there to reset our compass to true North.' That phrase refers to more than just sharpening one's investment skills.*"- Zurk Botha, owner of Zurk Botha Associates (Pty) Ltd, a South African Independent Financial Advisory Practice. Seven-time Berkshire Hathaway attendee.

"Going to the shareholders' meeting and sitting in the arena, it dawned on me after listening intently to the two of them, Charlie Munger and Warren Buffett for I think six hours… that investing is actually pure common sense."- Mel Meltzer, financial adviser for Platinum Portfolios, a South African independent owner-managed fund management company. Three-time Berkshire attendee.

"Saying it is one thing and doing it is another. That's where my fascination with Warren and Charlie started. They have done it over a period of 60 years: they have consistently done what they said they would do, and I think that's almost unique in the world. I don't think there's any other institution that I know of that is able to do that over such a long period of time. You put them up there and you try and emulate what they've done."- Piet Viljoen, Executive Director and Portfolio Manager of Counterpoint Asset Manager, a South African-based multi-strategy asset management business. Six-time Berkshire Hathaway AGM attendee.

CHARLIE, OH CHARLIE

28th November, a day perhaps like any other day
Except that the world lost you.
People pass everyday
And yet some passings are hugely profound
Like your passing
Leaving a gaping abyss
Not only for your loved ones
Not only for your friends
Not only for Warren
For whom you are irreplaceable
But too, for the multitude who respected
Your brilliance
Your wisdom
Your teachings
Born out of the Renaissance man that you were
A modern day example of embracing all knowledge
Developing yourself as much as possible
Whether it be mathematics
Science or Architecture
Philosophy
You schooled yourself
By reading. And by God, did you read.
Good decision-making should rest across disciplines
You said
Lifelong learning is paramount to long-term success
You said
I don't give a damn what someone else has
You said
Spend less than you earn

You said
The best armor of old age
Is a well spent life preceding it
You said.
Charlie, oh Charlie
You said so much over the years
Teaching people
Guiding people
Setting a fine example
Preaching about the power of inversion
Making an extraordinary
Amount of money
By investing in an old fashion way
Along with Warren Buffett
Your longtime friend
Business partner
His right-hand man
His confidante,
You were until the very end.
There was no one on the planet
Who could size up a deal faster
Spotting rare opportunities
And stepping up to the pie counter
To load up
Seizing unfair advantages with glee
Charlie, oh Charlie
You will live on
Long after most of us have passed
Through your legacy
Through your writings
Through the umpteen examples
Of the fine man that you were
Treading this earth
For 99 years and 47 weeks.

- Jackie Aylett
29 November 2023

Image source: https://aayushbhaskar.com/charlie-munger/

The contents of this book were composed over a period of three years. It is important to note that the ages, statistics, and net worth figures contained herein were recorded in real-time. We believe that this provides a reliable and accurate representation of the data available at the time of writing.

The author and publishers have made all reasonable efforts to contact copyright-holders for permission, and apologize for any omissions or errors in the form of credit given. Corrections may be made to future printings.

First published by Kimon Sarandos Aylett
© 2023 Kimon Sarandos Aylett

978-0-7961-2772-3 | Sex Before 80 | Paperback
978-0-7961-2773-0 | Sex Before 80 | Ebook

Interior formatting by Gregg Davies Media
(www.greggdavies.com)

All rights reserved
The moral right of the author has been asserted.
No part of this publication may be reproduced, distributed, or transmitted in any form or by any means, including photocopying, recording, or other electronic or mechanical methods, without the prior written permission of the author, except in the case of brief quotations embodied in critical reviews and certain other non-commercial uses permitted by copyright law.

TABLE OF CONTENTS

The Beginning	12
Buffett Cornerstone	22
Chapter 1 – Reputation	33
Chapter 2 – Aylett & Company Fund Managers	60
Chapter 3 – Heroes	66
Chapter 4 – Charlie	74
Chapter 5 – Choosing the Right Partner	90
Chapter 6 – Woodstock for Capitalists	106
Chapter 7 – Like-minded, Focused Individuals	150
Chapter 8 – Rational Thinking	164
Chapter 9 – Circle of Competence	171
Chapter 10 – Curveball	180
Chapter 11 – Get Rich SLOW	188
Chapter 12 – Tap Dancing to Work	200
Berkshire 2023	210
Afterword	212
About the Author	215
References	216

Special thanks to Aylett and Company Fund Managers for backing my vision & the story.

• • • • • • • • • • •

This book is dedicated to my parents and two younger brothers, whom I love to the stars and back.

You are about to embark on a journey toward better investing and decision-making. May you also arrive at a better understanding of life.

"Charlie, oh Charlie, You will live on"

• • • • • • • • • • •

On 28 November 2022, we sent a copy of the manuscript to both Warren Buffett & Charlie Munger.

Warren replied promptly via his assistant, Debbie Bosanek.

Dear Walter and Kimon,

"You two have come up with a very imaginative book. And Charlie and I certainly appreciate you making the long trek to the Berkshire meeting.

Roger Federer is definitely the real deal and a very close friend of my good friend, Jorge Paulo Lemann. Jorge Paulo played at Wimbledon and, though well into his 80s, is no one to challenge at tennis.

Good luck to both of you."

Before I started writing, I was advised by my dad to 'dip' into the following books to gain an improved understanding of Warren Buffett and Charlie Munger. Most quotes and references in this book originate from them. I highly recommend this book list for anyone wanting to improve their insight into Buffett's wisdom and Charlie's brilliant anecdotes.

I can assure you that the return on investment of your time will be more than worthwhile.

- Poor Charlie's Almanack: The Wit and Wisdom of Charles T. Munger, by Peter D. Kaufman.
- Warren Buffett: The Making of an American Capitalist, by Roger Lowenstein.
- The Snowball: Warren Buffett and the Business of Life, by Alice Schroeder.
- Damn Right: Behind the Scenes with Berkshire Hathaway Billionaire Charlie Munger; by Janet Lowe.

THE BEGINNING

- The Beginning -

There are two types of families.

FAMILY 1:

Little Jimmy comes home from school crying, runs to his room, and shuts the door. His father goes to Jimmy to find out what's wrong.

> J : I hate Michael! I wish he were dead!
> F : Excuse me?
> J : You heard me! Damn, Michael!
> F : Who's this Michael boy? And what did he do to you?
> J : He's the class bully and was mean to me!
> F : I see. So, what exactly happened, my boy?
> J : We were on the playground playing hand tennis. He lost and was a bad loser! He then started making fun of me and said mean words to me! It made me so angry! I had no comebacks, and all the kids were laughing at me!
> F : I see. And how did you react to all of this?
> J : I couldn't say anything; my words were lost — my heart felt like little knives were cutting through it. I started crying and ran off!
> F : I'm sorry to hear that, Son.
> J : I wish Michael were DEAD!
> F : Now, now, let's take a step back and reassess the situation, shall we?
> J : How should I have reacted, Dad? Should I have fought back and said something mean to him? Every word he said made me feel weak and useless!

At this point in the conversation, Jimmy's father leaves the room. Soon after, he returns with a small black book in his hand. He hands the book to his son and explains that the answers to his son's questions are all in there.

J: You're saying I need to read this whole book to work out how to deal with my class bully?

F: Well, not the whole book, just a small part. You can pick any 'chapter' you want, in any order, and apply the lessons in it to a relevant life struggle or situation. I promise you; it always works.

J: Like?

F: Well, according to Leviticus 19:18, one should not take revenge on others or bear grudges, continue to hate them but love your neighbors as you love yourself.

The little black book in the boy's hands was The Bible.

FAMILY 2:

Little Benjamin comes home crying from school, runs to his room, and shuts the door. His father goes to Benjamin to find out what's wrong.

B: I hate Michael! I wish he were dead!

F: Excuse me?

B: You heard me! Damn, Michael!

F: Who's this Michael boy? And what did he do to you?

B: He's the class bully! He was mean to me today!

F: I see. Tell me what happened, my boy.

B: We received our weekly math test results today. I didn't do too well. Michael started making fun of me and said really mean words to me! It made me so angry! I had no comebacks, and all the kids were laughing at me!

F: I see, and how did you react to all of this?

B: I couldn't say anything; my words were lost – my heart felt so sore, Dad. I started crying and ran out of the classroom.

F: I'm sorry to hear that, Son.

B: I wish Michael were DEAD!

F: Now, now. Let's calm down. Let's take a step back and reassess the situation.

B: How should I have reacted, Dad? Should I have fought back and said something mean to him? Every word he said made me feel weak and useless!

At this point in the conversation, Benjamin's father leaves the room. Soon after, he returns with a small black book in his hand. He hands the book to his son and explains that the answers to his son's questions are all there.

B: You're saying I need to read this whole book to work out how to deal with my class bully?
F: Well, not the whole book, just a small part. You can pick any 'chapter' in any order and apply the lessons in it to a relevant life struggle or situation.
B: Like?
F: Well, according to Warren Buffett, Page 22, you can always tell him to go to hell tomorrow. Tom Murphy, a Berkshire director, gave Mr. Buffett this great piece of advice years ago on the importance of recognizing and controlling your emotions. Holding your tongue is the smartest thing to do in a fiery situation. Don't erupt in a moment of anger and risk saying something you may regret. Words cannot be taken back. Walk away, cool off, and tell Michael to go to hell if you still feel the same way tomorrow.

You will continue to suffer if you react emotionally to everything said to you. Real power means sitting back and observing things with magic. Real power is restraint. If words control you, that means everyone else can control you. Breathe and allow things to pass.

The little black book in the boy's hands was *The Snowball: Warren Buffett and the Business of Life*, a biography of Warren Buffett by Alice Schroeder.

You can guess which type of family I belonged to.

I grew up in an 'investment family'. My mother worked for several investment companies, as did my father. My parents dreamed of creating a legacy for their three sons, and in 2005, they set up their own investment company, Aylett & Company Fund Managers. Even our dogs formed part of this investment family; our Beagle was named Munger, after Charlie Munger – partner of Warren Buffett, a world-renowned investment guru. It is, therefore, understandable that I, from a young age, became familiar with the investment world.

Personally, the central focus of this investment world has been my father, with my mother playing a crucial role during the early years of my father's 'apprenticeship' and the establishment of Aylett & Co. My parents started as co-founders – which developed into a journey toward better investment, decision-making, and understanding of life. My father's admiration for Charlie Munger and Warren Buffett greatly influenced the nature of that journey. Let me share some background on these two investment 'rock stars'.

FIRST THINGS FIRST. WHO IS WARREN BUFFETT?

Some know him as the Oracle of Omaha, and others associate him with all the billionaire investors of Wall Street. To my mind, he is nothing less than the tortoise to the Wall Street hare. Buffett is a US billionaire investor, Chairman, and CEO of Berkshire Hathaway, an American multinational conglomerate holding company headquartered in Omaha, Nebraska.

His trusted partner and right-hand man is Charlie Munger, who has served as Vice-Chairman of Berkshire Hathaway since 1978. Over 40,000 people attend Berkshire's annual general meeting in Omaha, referred to by some as Woodstock for Capitalists. At the AGM, Buffett, and Munger talk about investing and share good, old-fashioned folksy wisdom.

Buffett is the talker. He is an entertainer and self-chronicler who bought his first stock at the tender age of eleven. Consistently relaxed and self-effacing, he often mocks himself for being a poor dresser. He enjoys sharing vignettes from his career, with a compulsion to tell and retell and to mythologize his past (Lowenstein, 1997:293).

Buffett is known to spend six hours of his day reading; while drinking five to six Coca-Colas. He often jokes that he is one-quarter Coca-Cola: the drink accounts for 25 percent of his daily calorie intake. Amusingly, Buffett's money follows his mouth as Berkshire Hathaway owns about 10 percent of Coca-Cola, a stake worth around $22 billion. He doesn't own a computer and opts to use a flip phone rather than a smartphone. Buffett is said to be always level-headed and a gentleman. He is close friends with Bill Gates, and the pair make a lethal bridge partnership. Bridge is known as "the game of a lifetime" because it is impossible to master. Even after playing bridge for years and years, you'll always discover new challenges and continue to learn. I can imagine this tickling the fancy of Buffett and Gates!

Buffett has an extensive track record of beating the stock market. He hangs a public speaking certificate rather than his college degree in his office. He is 92 years old and has lived in the same five-bedroom house in Omaha, purchased in 1956 for $31,500. It is rumored that he has only sent one email in his life – to Jeff Raikes of Microsoft.

Buffett had an estimated net worth of $103 billion when writing this book as of August 2022.

THE NEXT THING, OF COURSE, IS WHO IS CHARLIE MUNGER?

Our Beagle was named after Charlie Munger, an American billionaire investor, businessman, and former real estate attorney. He is Vice-Chairman of Berkshire Hathaway. Charlie was not only Buffett's business partner and close friend; in today's terms, Charlie and Warren have shared a decade-long 'bromance'. Charlie was also born in Omaha,

Nebraska. In his early teens, he worked at Buffett & Son, a grocery store owned by Warren Buffett's grandfather. Charlie is famously known to be a disciple of Benjamin Franklin, an American polymath and one of the Founding Fathers of the United States.

While Warren Buffett is arguably one of most admired and famous investors to have walked Wall Street, Charlie Munger has purposefully sidestepped the limelight, preferring relative anonymity instead. Warren will often lead in answering questions at the Berkshire Hathaway AGM. Warren will turn to his partner, "Anything to add, Charlie?" Charlie will grumble his famous line, "I have nothing to add."

The way people describe Charlie is sometimes how I describe my dad. They are both rather blunt, enjoy giving sermons on their soapboxes, and believe that their answer is right or is the most logical or rational view. Growing up, my dad quoted Charlie Munger often in the context of some family discussion. My brothers and I grew so accustomed to this that Charlie Munger seemed like a familiar, old uncle to us.

More on Charlie and his 'Mungerisms' later in the book.

・・・・・・・・・・・

30 April 2022, Omaha, Nebraska, CHI Health Center Arena, Berkshire Hathaway Annual General Meeting 09:00 a.m.

At the naïve age of 26, I am one of the 40,000 Buffett disciples at the Berkshire Hathaway AGM. Hundreds of languages and accents can be heard throughout the CHI Health Center Arena. I wonder, *"Why would all these individuals travel worldwide to watch two grandpas chat ball for eight hours while they drink Coke and eat See's Candies?"*

Three levels below the Berkshire gathering is an adjoining 200,000-square-foot exhibition hall where dozens of Berkshire subsidiaries have set up booths to sell their products. From See's Candies to Justin Boots, the rich diversity of Berkshire's subsidiaries can be overwhelming. These subsidiaries are evaluated for shareholders by Warren and Charlie, while downstairs, fiercely being consumed by countless Berkshire attendees, most of them making a beeline for See's Candies that must sell tons of its famous peanut brittle and salty, nutty candy on the day. This cycle continues throughout the day as individuals rotate between the exhibition hall and the auditorium.

A short film starts the meeting. The Berkshire 'movie' shows humorous clips of Warren and Charlie interspersed with advertisements for Berkshire's various subsidiaries, including cameos by famous actors or celebrities. The crowd roars in applause following each commercial. The film concludes. The crowd gradually quietens, and the lights dim. An announcer alerts the crowd, "And now, the two legends you all have traveled thousands of miles to see… give a warm Omaha welcome to Warren Buffett and Charlie Munger!"

After this buildup, one could be forgiven for expecting Warren and Charlie to come running onto the stage, performing cartwheels, accompanied by smoke and light effects, and for the pair to do the typical motivational speaker introduction, "Good morning, Omaha! Man, oh man, can we feel your energy today!" followed by running through the crowd and high-fiving people. Instead, two gentle, elderly men unhurriedly slip through a small opening in the stage curtain, taking their sweet time to reach their seats.

With a crack of a Coca-Cola can being opened, Warren takes a quick sip and grunts, *"Thank you, and good morning. That's Charlie, and I'm Warren. You can tell us apart because he can hear, and I can see. That's why we work together so well. We each have our specialty."*

I had a sudden surge of déjà vu. I had experienced this moment before. Ah, yes. This would be my third time hearing Warren mutter that opening line.

You may be wondering how a 26-year-old from South Africa ended up attending his third Berkshire AGM

Over 40,000 Berkshire disciples at the 2022 Berkshire Hathaway Annual General Meeting.

Let's backtrack to how my father accidentally became a Chartered Accountant; through my mother, who got drawn into the investment world in 1997. Subsequently, he went on to join Coronation Fund Managers, a boutique investment house in Cape Town, South Africa.

BUFFETT CORNERSTONE

"I went to Berkshire to find the holy grail to investing, which also turned out to be the holy grail to life." - Walter Aylett

After being told that he should become a plumber by a career guidance counselor, receiving minus six percent for mathematics in his final year of school, failing at two universities, spending a year abroad in Portugal, and finally catching a massive wakeup call during his two-year military service, Walter finally grew up, much to his parent's relief. He had the initiative to take out a student loan and register for a Bachelor of Commerce degree at the then University of Port Elizabeth, or UPE, in the city where he grew up.

Years later, this was renamed Nelson Mandela University. He met his future wife, Jackie, in class, and the pair would battle it out competitively throughout the completion of their degree programs.

A mishap with an interview would change the course of Walter's life. He had been flown to Johannesburg by a blue chip South African mining company, supposedly to apply for a job in Human Resources.

When he arrived for the interview, he was only to find that the company was not actually recruiting for that position.

To keep him occupied until his flight back to Port Elizabeth, the company arranged for him to spend the day with their financial director. He dispensed valuable advice to the young Walter on the merits of having a Chartered Accounting qualification.

A further incident around that time cemented Walter's decision to become a Chartered Accountant.

While waiting for his postgraduate interview with the Industrial Relations professor, Walter browsed through several companies reports lying on the coffee table outside the professor's office.

What struck him immediately was that the captains of the industry running these companies were either qualified as Chartered Accountants, graduates of the prestigious Masters in Business Administration (MBA) program, or lawyers.

Here, Walter realized that he needed something extra behind his name. He was admitted as an articled clerk at a small firm in his home town, Port Elizabeth. Known as the Windy City, it is a somewhat drab town on South Africa's East Coast. My parents married in 1988 and moved to Cape Town a year later, a more sought after place to live.

After completing his articles, my dad took a year off work to complete his Honors degree in Accounting while my mom, Jackie, worked in Client Liaison with Allan Gray Investment Counsel, a prestigious investment firm in Cape Town. Jackie would often bring work home to review her clients' investment portfolios, and Walter quickly became fascinated with the idea that people were paid to invest other people's money.

Walter passed the grueling Board Exam in 1992 set by the South African Institute of Chartered Accountants (SAICA) and celebrated mischievously with a few of his fellow graduates by swimming in the well known Adderley Street fountain in Cape Town. His dad, Joe, was convinced Walter had paid someone to pass him! His proud Greek mom, Katina, shouted her husband down. With Walter now a Chartered Accountant, he and Jackie worked in London before backpacking in Thailand.

They visited relatives in Australia and returned to South Africa in 1994 after the assassination of Chris Hani, the then leader of the South African Communist Party and Chief of Staff of Umkhonto We Sizwe, the Armed Wing of the African National Congress (ANC). It was a daunting time for any young South African heading homeward.

Hani was assassinated by Janusz Waluś, a Polish immigrant, during the unrest leading up to the transition to democracy. His assassination marked a turning point in South Africa, and there were deep fears that the country would erupt into violence. Although he was not yet president, Nelson Mandela appealed for calm in what was regarded as a presidential speech.

Tonight, I am reaching out to every South African, black and white, from the very depths of my being. A white man, full of prejudice and hate, came into our country and committed a deed so foul that our whole nation now teeters on the brink of disaster. A white woman, of Afrikaner origin, risked her life so that we may know, and bring to justice, this assassin. The cold-blooded murder of Chris Hani has sent shock waves throughout the country and the world. Now is the time for all South Africans to stand together against those who, from any quarter, wish to destroy what Chris Hani gave his life for - the freedom of us all (text as it appears on the ANC website).

Claiming political motivation for their crimes and saying that they had acted on the orders of the Conservative Party, Hani's killers appeared before the Truth and Reconciliation Commission (TRC), a court-like justice body instituted in South Africa after the end of apartheid. George Bezos, human rights activist and anti-apartheid lawyer represented the Hani family. The TRC ruled that they had not acted on orders and denied their applications.

Bezos had represented Nelson Mandela at the Rivonia Trial in the mid-60s, the trial that led to the 27-year imprisonment of Nelson Mandela, convicted of sabotage. Bezos's defense of Nelson Mandela is largely credited with saving him from the death penalty. This Greek South African who had, as a teenager, come to South Africa as a refugee died on the ninth of September 2020, aged 92. He was given a state funeral at the Greek Orthodox Church in Johannesburg, where the pre- eminent defense lawyer of the Struggle was remembered as a man who never forgot his proud Greek heritage and was always committed to doing the right thing.

George Bezos was Greek. I am proudly of Greek heritage. There's something to be said for remarkable nonagenarian individuals like Bezos, Charlie Munger, and Warren Buffett, who have excelled in their respective fields of passion. Not sure what nonagenarian means? Neither did I! It refers to people between 90 and 99 years old, Exhibit A: Mr. Buffett, Exhibit B: Mr. Munger.

To return to the story at hand. It was a brave move for Walter and Jackie to return home in March 1994 during extreme political uncertainty. Jackie was hired in a senior management position by Old Mutual, one of a handful of female executives employed by the company in the mid-1990s.

Walter was no longer interested in working as a Chartered Accountant. From the time he learned about asset management through Jackie's work at Allan Gray and through his exposure to her network of investment professionals, he developed a keen interest in the investing field.

Walter's path toward becoming a fund manager started when he had an offer to work at Syfrets Managed Assets in June 1994. Whereas in London, he had worked for an investment firm in the back office, now, he was appointed as a financial manager - not as an investment analyst, but he was still part of asset management.

He started studying for a Chartered Financial Analyst (CFA) qualification, a postgraduate professional certification offered internationally by the American-based CFA institute to investment and financial professionals.

I became aware that to be an analyst or fund manager was very hard because these positions were sought after. That's where the money was. In my case, I realized that I had a passion for it, a passion for finding undiscovered assets or gems.

I used to collect wine and loved reading up on South African wines and finding ones that hadn't yet been discovered, and that later became very popular.

I loved gardening, which was like a form of investing. You plant a tree in the right place, and it bears fruit. Those were the dividends.

My role at Syfrets would gradually shift toward the investment side of things, and I would find myself sitting in weekly investment meetings led by the main boss, Jan Kuiper. Kuiper had a substantial investment background from a stockbroker firm, Ivor Jones (Roy & Co), which later became known as Deutsche Bank in South Africa. I respected Jan; he was very good to me. He allowed me to move away from being a financial manager to becoming an investment analyst, my first lucky break in life. I ended up working with a guy called Tim Allsop, who turned out to be one of SA's best fund managers.

For four years I worked at Syfrets and was very successful with Tim. We focused mainly on small companies, and my accounting experience stood me in good stead - Walter Aylett.

Through Kuiper, Walter first heard of Warren Buffett. On numerous occasions, he recalled that Jan would go on 'Buffett' tangents. Intrigued by his boss's repeated references to this man from Omaha, Walter started reading up on Buffett.

1997 saw Walter's career path take a new direction when Coronation Fund Managers headhunted him. This was his second break. Coronation was a big hitter in the South African investment scene.

The move brought a great deal of change into Walter's life. There were new bosses, competitive colleagues, and fund mandates of a substantial size. Yet, in a sense, it was like going home. In 1993, fifteen employees walked out on Syfrets and formed Coronation.

Walter excelled at Coronation for the next eight years, starting a special technology fund and managing the Optimum Growth Fund, a world-wide flexible fund. He was known as a maverick and single-handedly managed the two funds. Today, the Optimum Growth Fund is run by an investment manager backed by 25 analysts and fund managers!

Walter's interest in Buffett remained constant in this time of flux. He was determined to find out more about the 'Oracle of Omaha', so he approached his new boss with a rather cheeky proposal. Walter suggested Coronation send him and some colleagues to Omaha, Nebraska, to attend a Berkshire Hathaway Shareholders Annual General Meeting.

It was not so much the company that drew Walter but rather knowing that this would allow him to hear Buffett talk.

His colleagues could not fathom why he would travel thousands of kilometers to listen to an old man grumble into a microphone while guzzling down Cherry Coke, but Walter wasn't taking no for an answer.

After numerous attempts at persuading his seniors, he eventually received the green light. He truly believed that the holy grail of investing lay in the American Midwest in Omaha.

Walter was accompanied by fellow fund manager and colleague Kokkie Koyman, who backed his belief. Walter and Kokkie would be part of the first South Africans to attend a Berkshire AGM and listen to Charlie Munger and Warren Buffett.

The two 'Saffas'[1] would join 7,700 fellow Buffett stakeholders at the 1999 AGM.

Here follows Walter's description of his first visit to a Berkshire Hathaway AGM, where he first met Buffett and Munger. He was particularly impressed by Charlie's forthrightness and his message about the basic principles of investing, common sense, and rationality.

---

1. A "Saffa" is a colloquial expression for a person from South Africa.

At my first AGM, I didn't know who Charlie Munger was. The AGM was much smaller than it is today. It was held in a tiny place and was very intimate and shareholder focused.

It consisted mainly of industry questions. There wasn't much about esoteric stuff. No laughing and even less life advice and more about insurance and industrial investments held by Berkshire Hathaway. That was the start of 19 or 20 visits. This happened every May.

So, there's this guy. Warren's partner, his pal, as he calls him, Charlie Munger. Something made me realize that this was an exceptional man. Not much had been written about him yet. At that stage, there were no books on Charlie.

Later on, Damn Right! And Poor Charlie's Almanack came out – two world-class books.

These two men just made so much sense. It became clear that the process of going there wasn't only to listen to them but to meet other like-minded people and to learn about the philosophy of life. You know how you deal with problems and how you make successful decisions as an individual.

I loved the experience. I thought it was the greatest privilege. You reset the compass to true North every year. You clear the windscreen. You remind yourself of the basic principles of investing, which is common sense and being rational.

The more I heard Charlie speak, the more I heard this message of education, of being rational. He certainly espouses a stoic philosophy; you know, take it on the chin. Don't feel sorry for yourself.

I can be cynical and curt. I cut through the bullshit. Charlie is like that and gets away with it due to his brilliant mind and his professional success.

I don't think he is intentionally nasty; I just don't think he suffers fools gladly. On the other hand, Buffett is the Dale Carnegie guy. Everyone wants to be his friend.

It was clear that Walter wasn't attending the AGM intending to invest in Berkshire but rather due to a yearning to learn how to make money from the Masters of Investing.

Walter had pioneered a revolutionary investment practice that, in hindsight, was quite extraordinary. His annual Berkshire excursions would attract top seniors at Coronation, like-minded clients, and captains of industry.

It coincided with the boom of the internet and media and international investment opportunities for South Africa.

This virgin voyage into the land of cowboy hats, steaks and peanut brittle bars would become a yearly occurrence for Walter over the next 20 years.

The only difference was that the group of South Africans would get bigger, and the Berkshire attendees would grow exponentially.

Walter's visits to Omaha made him miss nearly every Mother's Day in South Africa, with Jackie kept very busy looking after three active little boys. He would return from these trips loaded with See's Candies, toys for his sons, and special gifts for his wife. He did not doubt that he was getting closer to understanding the holy grail of investing, which also turned out to be the holy grail of life. With all the challenges he would face as an individual, Walter is convinced that he would never have been able to cope if he had not encountered Buffett and Munger.

2004 saw Walter move in a direction that required courage, confidence and independence. After seven years at Coronation, he was happy but not entirely satisfied. He wanted to be the captain of his own custom-made ship, to choose a crew he respected, and chart his own course through the stock market seas.

He wanted to start his own asset management house and prove to himself that he could play the investment game with like-minded people to create a company that would be run the Buffett way.

I had no reason to leave Coronation. It was a well-paying job. I was left to manage my own funds. But as Buffett said, you want to get out of bed excited; you want to tap dance to work. I felt that you prove yourself when you're really good at something and have done it on your own.

Several years of absorbing Buffett and Charlie's wisdom would guide Walter through some of the most grueling months of his investment career.

Despite extraordinary inefficiencies in registering as a Financial Services Provider, my parents, Walter and Jackie, persevered so that my dad could realize his dream of owning his own asset management company.

He would use one of Buffett's most important principles: *Reputation*.

Walter and fellow South Africans with Warren Buffett and Charlie Munger at the Berkshire Hathaway AGM 2005. First left Thys Visser (deceased CEO of Remgro), forth left Thys du Toit (ex-CEO of Coronation Fund Managers), Kokkie Koyman (Executive director and portfolio manager at Denker Capital), Walter Aylett, Laurie Dippenaar (ex-CEO FirstRand group) and Piet Viljoen (Executive Director and Portfolio Manager of Counterpoint Asset Manager)

CHAPTER 1 – REPUTATION

"It takes 20 years to build a reputation and five minutes to ruin it."
- Warren Buffett

During the market crisis of 1987, Warren Buffett made an unprecedented move. Investing $700 million in bond trading powerhouse Salomon Brothers, Warren bought a 12 percent holding in the American investment bank making Berkshire Hathaway their biggest shareholder. Many close to Buffett were surprised at the investment decision due to his general criticism of investment bankers and their greed. Salomon Brothers were considered 'one of the club' – one of the Wall Street rats. Charlie Munger did not like their culture and often disparagingly compared bankers to heroin addicts because they could not control themselves.

Shortly after Warren and Charlie joined the Salomon board, things exploded. 1991 witnessed a scandal that rocked Wall Street. Salomon Brothers had been accused of improper trading of treasury bonds. The company had exceeded the limit for trading government bonds. The United States Treasury, Federal Reserve, the Securities and Exchange Commission, and the Department of Justice were collectively investigating Salomon Brothers. The company owed $150 billion: the most any private company owed at the time in the United States.

Buffett met with the head of the Federal Reserve of New York, Nick Brady, the town sheriff. Buffett conveyed that he had never really owed a lot of money in his life other than a little mortgage on his house and that $150 billion was simply staggering. He hoped that he would have a few weeks to breathe. To his dismay, the sheriff stated that the Salomon Brothers, Berkshire, and Buffett should prepare for any eventuality.

In days to come, the US Department of Treasury would suspend Salomon Brothers from participating in the auction of new issues: the town sheriff had essentially arrested the neighborhood burglar. This was a milestone turning period for Buffett, who feared his reputation would forever be on the line. He had 24 hours to either move forward or bow out.

Salomon Brothers was on the verge of bankruptcy. Buffett rolled up his sleeves, stepped up, and took responsibility.

Buffett stepped in as interim Chairman and Chief Executive of the besieged company for an annual salary of $1. He felt this was necessary to gain information regarding the company's history and was committed to doing everything he could to make things right for the future; failing was not an option.

After meetings with lawyers, councils and board members, furious fellow Salomon employees would exit the building in limos and private cars. Buffett, meanwhile, would ride the subway back to his hotel downtown.

After receiving the death knell from Mr. Brady, Buffett was essentially pleading for his life. His voice cracking with strain and tension, Warren uttered, "Nick, this is the most important day of my life." Unsure if what Buffett was saying was correct, Brady sensed that Buffett truly felt and meant what he was saying. The treasury modified its order with an endorsement of Buffett, which saved Salomon Brothers. Brady went with Buffett because he trusted him, as Munger put it.

It shows how having a good reputation is really helpful in life – (Warren Buffett, HBO Documentary, Becoming Warren Buffett (1:03:59)).

Buffett would appear before the Telecommunications and Finance subcommittee of the Energy and Commerce Committee of the US House of Representatives. Here is an extract of the opening statement from his Salomon Brothers testimony.

Mr. Chairman, I thank you for the opportunity to appear before this subcommittee. I would like to start by apologizing for the acts that have brought us here. The nation has a right to expect its rules and laws to be obeyed…

… My job is to deal with both the past and the future. The past actions of

Salomon are presently causing our 8,000 employees and their families to bear a stain. Virtually all these employees are hardworking, able, and honest. I want to find out exactly what happened in the past so that this stain is borne by the guilty few and removed from the innocent…

… I also have asked every Salomon employee to be his or her own compliance officer. After they first obey all rules, I then want employees to ask themselves whether they are willing to have any contemplated act appear the next day on the front page of their local paper, to be read by their spouses, children, and friends, with the reporting done by an informed and critical reporter. If they follow this test, they need not fear my other message to them: Lose money for the firm, and I will be understanding; lose a shred of reputation for the firm, and I will be ruthless (Buffett, 1991).

What saved Salomon was the backing of a man of integrity whose reputation was bulletproof.

Like Buffett, Walter was to face his own nemesis when embarking on a new investment. He was to experience a similar 'Salomon Brothers moment' in his fight to establish Aylett & Company Fund Managers.

TANGLE WITH THE FINANCIAL SERVICES BOARD

To start an investment company requires a license to operate as a Financial Services Provider (FSP). Aylett & Co obtained FSP authorization from the Financial Services Board (FSB) without a hitch. This was the green light to start attracting and managing funds under management. Without warning, a facsimile (yes, that long ago) was sent by the FSB informing the fledgling company that their FSP license had been withdrawn with no reason given.

What followed could have come straight from a Franz Kafka novel with absurd and nonsensical twists and turns. What? Oh, I get it; you're probably wondering who the hell this Franz Kafka is! You could ask my 84-year-old maternal grandmother, who knows all about literature, or you could Google it. Better yet, let me tell you.

Franz Kafka regarded as one of the most important figures of 20th-century literature, was a Bohemian novelist and short story writer. His characters often faced absurd situations like in 'the trial', where a man is charged with a crime that is never named.

Kafkaesque comes from Franz Kafka's surname and describes a difficult situation that feels surreal, almost like a nightmare. My granny said straight up that the whole FSB license withdrawal was a fiasco, totally Kafkaesque. She was so right.

The dockmaster initially gave my father the license to embark on his voyage. Days later, a fellow dockworker reported to the dockmaster with nautical rumors stating that Walter had been involved with pirates of some sort and, therefore, should not be allowed his license to voyage. The license was shortly withdrawn, and an investigation commenced. Aylett & Co's sails had billowed with promise, then collapsed in the blink of an eye.

Walter's license to invest was withdrawn due to the accusation that he had been involved in inside trading after a large trade in 2000 was made by Coronation Fund Managers. At the time, the FSB conducted a full and thorough investigation, and Walter and Coronation were cleared of any wrongdoing.

Following the blow dealt by the FSB, my parents' lives were turned upside down with several months of sleepless nights. Lawyers, long phone calls, whispering behind closed doors, and invasion of their privacy became the order of the day.

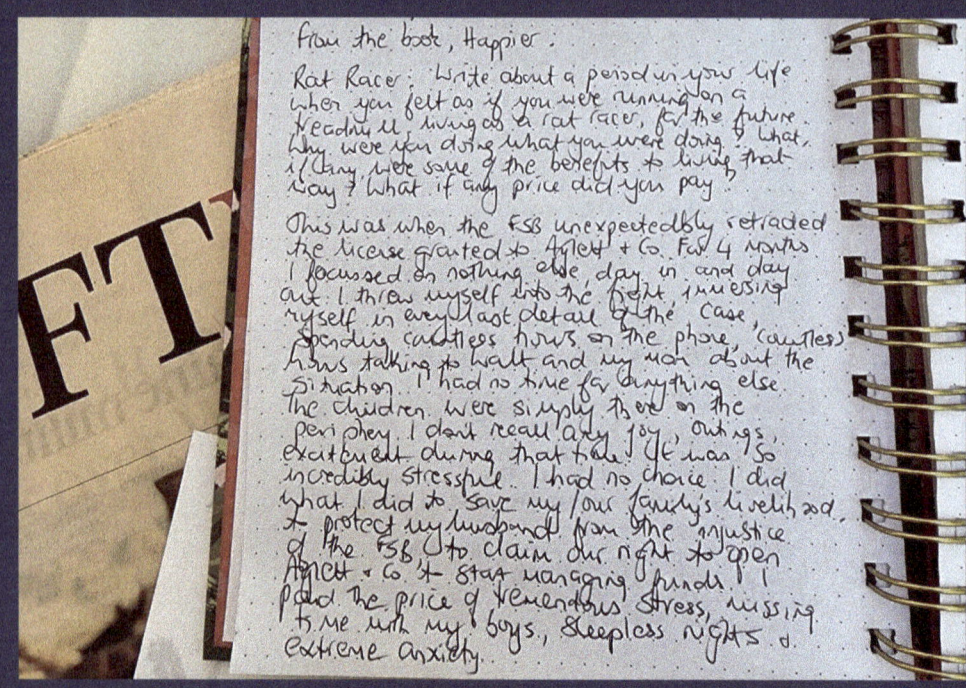

This is a passage taken from my mother's journal back in 2005. It provides a glimpse into the struggles that my parents, particularly my mother, had to endure during the FSB period. The entry is a poignant reminder of the challenges they faced and the emotional turmoil they experienced during that time.

Walter knew his reputation was spotless and that he had done no wrong. He is an ethical investor who plays by the rules. What mattered was whether this could be proved to the FSB.

The FSB was like a sniffer dog, looking into Walter's life, trying to find any evidence to justify their reasoning for not granting Aylett & Co a license to operate. His reputation was placed under a magnifying glass.

He realized that the FSB was not merely looking at possible insider trading but at any instance of lawbreaking. Both Walter's personal and business life were being interrogated.

As a nine-year-old, I remember a period when my parents had either their cellphones or the home phone glued to their ears all the time. Uncharacteristically, my two brothers and I received very little attention from our mom and dad at the time, but our wonderful housekeeper,

Princess, who was like a second mother to us, and our au pair, Penny, made sure we were well cared for.

I was angry and confused but mostly curious about what was causing my parents to 'ignore' their children to this extent. They were usually so caring and involved with our days, and I knew it was not intentional. Worse still, I could see my parents were stressed but had no idea what the cause might be. Little did I know that they were fighting for our livelihood.

Two months of this isolation and social distancing passed until one bright morning brought my dad into my bedroom. He sat me down, clearly wanting to talk to me about something important.

This 'alone time' with him was rare during that time. He started by saying that he was going to speak to me about an extremely important life lesson. I put down my Calvin & Hobbes book and hoped this would explain why my parents had been so distant.

Young man, you will learn that life is sometimes unfair and unreasonable. How you ensure that you prevail in life is by having an excellent reputation. It takes 20 years to build a reputation, and it takes five seconds to lose it. If the ball is close to the line, you call it out.

Operate in a manner that beats what the standards require. Pay your taxes, pay more than what your taxes are. No one can say bad things about you then. Reputation, my boy, is everything; and remember, if you tell the truth, you won't have to remember any lies. It's such a simple concept.

My dad's words were a lot for a nine-year-old to take in. Confused about what a tax was but understanding the tennis analogy, this conversation has always stuck in my mind.

The conversation would be referred to in an essay on integrity that my father had asked me to write during a job shadowing school assignment at his office when I was 17.

Why Integrity is so important?

Integrity is one of the most important attributes of a person, group of people, **business**, team, you name it integrity is number 1. Every body makes mistakes even the' **rich and famous.**' A Good example of poor integrity that affected '**The rich and famous**' was **The tiger wood** incident, where he lied to his wife and cheated on her, here we have one of the best golfers of all time and a very famous sportsman shatter his reputation of his life because of poor integrity. He has taking years to build this reputation of a brilliant golfer, good valued and loyal man and now all of that is thrown away due to one foolish decision, we all saw how bad he felt and the pain he was going through during the time when the truth was coming out.

Now he thinks was it really worth this...this ultimate nightmare I'm going through, was one night of pleasure WORTH all of this hell.'

Another example of a 'rich and famous' is Strauss Khan, this is more related to business reputation, but the story of how poor integrity lost Khans reputation is not to different to the one above about Tiger woods. They may have different consequences but in the end they are the same crime.

Dominique Strauss Khan
Is a French economist, lawyer, and politician, and a member of the French Socialist Party. Strauss-Kahn became the Managing Director of the International Monetary Fund (IMF) on 28 September 2007, with the backing of his country's president, Nicolas Sarkozy, and served in that role until his resignation on 18 May 2011.[

Just a week before the incident with the hotel maid happened, Dominique Strauss occupied probably the most respected financial position in the world, as head of the IMF. He now stands accused of allegedly sexually assaulting the woman who came to clean his hotel suite in New York. It would seem that this is not the first such incident of his stepping out of the marital boundaries.

Something that every person should

Need to know, the truth will ALWAYS come out. ALWAYS. It might take hours, days, months or years, but it will come out. If you occupy a leadership or management position, think carefully about the implications of what you do and say. At all times. Something done in what you think is the privacy of your hotel room may make international headlines in a few hours' time. This is a lesson Tiger Woods learnt to the detriment of his family and his career when his infidelity became known. J Arthur Brown, former head of Fidentia, is currently trying to avoid facing a court of law to answer for allegedly siphoning millions from various investment funds in South Africa. He is now accusing the prosecutors in his case of being prepared to stop at nothing to secure a conviction.

In the end the lesson to be learnt here is that honesty is the best policy The truth is like a sniffer dog and you are like the drug, it doesn't matter how hard you hide, run and dodge, truth will always find you.

A few weeks ago, I made a poster that said "My goal is to work at Aylett and CO" and put pictures of business men etc, my dad said that I should put one more thing on the poster: Integrity. That is what makes Aylett and co stand out from the rest.

An essay I wrote on integrity for my father while interning at Aylett & Co, 2013.

Thankfully, my writing skill has improved since then, and I hope you will look beyond the grammatical errors in a teenager's essay and appreciate what I was attempting to convey regarding the importance of integrity.

After months of hell and reams of defense documentation meticulously compiled by his wife, Jackie, the FSB was forced to conclude that Walter was indeed 'clean' and rightly deserved the investment license for his new company. Aylett & Company Fund Managers was ready to set sail.

My father had experienced first-hand the power of Buffett's principle of the importance of a good reputation. Most importantly, Aylett & Company Fund Managers would be born out of applying this principle in its founders' fight to launch the company against tremendous odds.

Its foundation would be built on reputation, ethics, energy and integrity; Aylett & Co's DNA is guarded by the bulletproof reputation established over the years.

Integrity and reputation had kept both Berkshire Hathaway and Aylett & Co alive.

Being ethical. There needs to be a huge area between everything you should do and everything you can do without getting into legal trouble. I don't think you should come anywhere near that line. We don't deserve much credit for this.

It helps us make more money. I'd like to believe that we'd do well even if it didn't work. But more often, we've made extra money from doing the right thing (Munger, 2006:87).

If it's close to the line, it's out. – Walter Aylett.

But what exactly is reputation? Consult a dictionary, and reputation is *defined as the general opinion of people about something or how much respect or admiration someone or something receives based on past behavior or character.*

Whether we like it or not, we all have a good or bad reputation, exceptional or mediocre, an invisible result of anything and everything we do.

A recent experience brought this home to me in an unexpected way. My mom and I were in London for the Laver Cup 2022, a men's tennis tournament between teams from Europe and the rest of the world.

Attending the Laver Cup was a dream we'd held since the event started in 2017. The tennis greats were there; Federer, Nadal, Djokovic and Murray, boasting 66 Grand Slam titles among them.

The young guns, Tsitsipas, Berrettini, Norrie, Sock, de Minaur, Fritz, Schwartzman and Tiafoe, added to the fantastic line-up of players making up Team Europe and Team World, captained by none other than John McEnroe and Björn Borg.

We had tickets for the Friday evening and Saturday afternoon sessions. Each captain decides the draw on the day preceding play, and we had no idea who we would see.

We had each secured a coveted black RF Laver Cup 2022 cap before the merchandise points sold out, and we couldn't wait for the event to begin!

· · · · · · · · · · · ·

My mom and I secured limited edition RF Laver Cup caps before they sold out!

The Friday draw was released while we attended the team practice matches on a Thursday afternoon. My heart somersaulted. Federer and Nadal would play Sock and Tiafoe in the doubles! This was Federer's last professional tennis match, as the maestro had recently decided to retire. To see Roger and Nadal take to the court in doubles was absolutely thrilling. Our seats were right behind Team Europe, and being so close to the players, seeing them fool around, talk strategy, and cheer each other on, was surreal. Once the match ended, more was to come.

The Laver Cup event organizers had put together a whole retirement send-off for Roger Federer to usher him out on a wave of well-wishes from cheering fans and supporters. Images on massive screens and the black tennis court showed Federer's memorable tennis highlights.

There was a surprise performance from Ellie Goulding, the well known British singer, who afterward tweeted. *Such a ridiculously HUGE honor to be present for the final professional match of Roger Federer. An extraordinary athlete and gentleman. No words can do his spectacular career justice.*

Rivals, tennis legends and ultimately friends. Roger Federer and Rafael Nadal team up for Team Europe in Roger's final professional tennis match of his career. What a way to end it?

- Reputation -

When Federer took to the court to say his goodbyes, there was so much emotion inside the 02 arena. Players, fans, celebrities, family and friends all joined to bid farewell to the greatest player ever. This man, who for over 20 years had kept the world riveted with his magnificent skill on the court, elegant athleticism, amazing talent, and impeccable style, stood before us, wracked by sobs, completely overcome. There was a touching moment when Federer and Nadal sat next to one another on a bench, both crying, and Roger placed his hand on Rafa's, in a gesture of deep friendship. Federer's mom and dad, his wife, Mirka, his twin girls and twin boys, his sister and others joined him, supporting him one last time on the court.

Roger embraces his wife, Mirka.

There were so many micro-moments and so many cameos playing out. The electricity between Roger and his fans, his heartfelt gratitude, his immense sorrow to leave his beloved career, his rivals bear hugging him, his family embracing him. Master of Ceremonies, Jim Courier, reiterated the enormous impact that Federer has had on tennis as a player, role model, and the world's best. Half South African, half Swiss, the former ball boy became the world's best player and a true study in reputation excellence.

Fans, celebrities and fellow competitors huddle around Roger, joining his final farewell.

Roger begins his court farewell walk. He took over 10 minutes to even start the walk after trembling and crying so much.

Bill Gates had this to say about Federer some years back. *It's no secret that Roger Federer is the greatest tennis player ever. As David Foster Wallace wrote, he is: 'one of those rare, preternatural athletes who appear to be exempt, at least in part, from certain physical laws.' He also seems exempt from the laws of aging. At 36, he's still winning Grand Slams with a combination of grace and grit. But not as many fans know about what Roger is doing off the court. Twice I've had the thrill of being his doubles partner to help raise money for his foundation, and we've become friends in the process. I've learned how sincerely Roger and his team are working to improve the life prospects for poor children—a mission that stems from his childhood visits to his mother's home country of South Africa and seeing extreme poverty first-hand. Roger knows that effective philanthropy, like great tennis, requires discipline and time. It will be a sad day for all of us fans when he hangs up his racket—but we can take comfort in knowing that he's committed to making the world a more equitable place* (TIME, 2018).

In 2018, Federer was named one of TIMES's 100 Most Influential People. He has made a difference to those who most need it through his foundation; he has inspired thousands of young tennis players around the world, and he has shown what it is to be a devoted husband and father, a gentleman, and a good sportsman with a goofy sense of humor to boot. None of this was planned.

As he said in his farewell speech, *I only wanted to play tennis and have fun with my friends.* What a great case study on reputation.

• • • • • • • • • • • • •

My mom and I sharing this out-of-world experience at the Laver Cup 2022. We've certainly shared many Federer moments together!

The story unexpectedly continued the following day. My mom and I were staying in Chelsea, and after getting in at three a.m. from the previous night's tennis extravaganza, we were struggling to get going. We had tickets to the Saturday session that started at one p.m., and it almost felt like an anti-climax after Friday night's high.

My mom suggested we pop over to Daylesford Organic to grab a coffee before catching the tube to Greenwich. For those not in the know, the café-deli is part of Daylesford Organic, one of the UK's most sustainable farms, fully committed to being organic.

It's a real food emporium and a great treat to visit. While waiting for our takeaway coffees, a man wearing a gorgeous pale blue cashmere sweater came up to me, complimenting me on my RF Laver Cup cap and asking if I'd been at the match the previous night.

I immediately realized he was Tom Hiddleston, the internationally famous actor who played Loki in the Marvel Cinematic Universe Thor, opposite Chris Hemsworth! Although I could hardly get the words out, I asked him if I could take a picture.

"Sorry, but I'm off duty. I'm Tom, by the way," he said before leaving.

My heart sank, and I felt bitterly disappointed. Loki is my youngest brother's all time favorite movie character, and I knew he would have been over the moon to see a selfie of me with Loki. Subconsciously, I also lost some respect for Tom Hiddleston. How could he take the time to come up to me to start a conversation and yet not have the time to take a quick selfie? In that instant, I lost some respect for the man.

Not a minute later, though, he was back. "Look, I felt really bad for what I said, and I asked myself if Roger Federer would have done the same, and I realized that he wouldn't have turned you down."

Next thing we were taking a selfie, Tom reached out to introduce himself to my mom, and we bonded over stories of the night before at the Laver Cup, seeing Federer's last match and farewell. It turns out Tom had also been there and had got to meet Roger Federer and had a picture taken with him, wearing the same gorgeous pale blue cashmere sweater! Google this to see that even Tom Hiddleston was a little star-struck.

My respect for Tom Hiddleston had been restored, and I got to give my brother, Dinos, the framed selfie of Loki and me for his 22nd birthday a few weeks later.

• • • • • • • • • • • •

Tom Hiddleston and I take a selfie after he had a 'Federer' moment.

Tom and Roger. The night before with Roger (Source: Instagram).

- Reputation -

These stories of my time in London wouldn't be complete without writing about the Queen's funeral that took place that week. Her Majesty, Queen Elizabeth II, guided her family and her country through unprecedented social changes, showing unwavering commitment through her record-breaking reign (Mills, 2022). On the day of her funeral, September 19, 2022, the entire British nation came to a standstill to witness the Queen's final journey to her resting place in Windsor, and it was said that more than half the planet tuned in to watch the state funeral.

What a further case in point of a person with an exemplary reputation.

A shop window showing respect to the late Queen. The detail in the shops was impeccable.

Cards, flowers and letters of tears from the Queen's people showered the bases of the trees in Hyde Park.

The Queen's Royal Guard. They carry out ceremonial duties, including providing the Sovereign's Escort for State and Royal occasions. They'll now be known as the King's Royal Guard.

The thought of building such a massively impressive reputation can be overwhelming. On this topic, I've gained deep insight from Don Miguel Ruiz's New York Times bestselling book, The Four Agreements. Following the author's powerful code of conduct: Be Impeccable With Your Word, Don't Take Anything Personally, Don't Make Assumptions, Always Do Your Best, I've found wonderful guidance for building a good sense of self and a solid reputation.

CHAPTER 2 – AYLETT & COMPANY FUND MANAGERS

"I wanted to tap dance to work, prove to myself that I could do it on my own, and choose kind like-minded people to work with."
- Walter Aylett.

1 APRIL 2005

The morning was crisp and sunny. A promise was in the air, and one could hear two young boys yelling at each other in a commotion. We lived in a lovely house in leafy Bishops Court, Cape Town, with a magnificent view of the back of Table Mountain. On that day, the dining room was a hive of activity with whiteboards, computers, papers upon papers, and a castle built of furniture and blankets. The two boys were Walter's sons, Nikos and Dinos. This was the first day of operations for Aylett & Company Fund Managers. At the time, Jackie, Walter's wife, came to the rescue and extracted the children. Nikos, outraged that the building of his 'castle' was interrupted, was told by his mom, "Your father is building a company in the dining room. You can build a castle in your bedroom."

I would stroll past the dining room and sneak peeks or try to pick up on the conversations. It didn't make sense to me that my parents would be operating out of our dining room after their struggle and sacrifice for this all-important license. Where was the fancy office? The other employees? The suits? Confused, I would retreat to the garden to practice my bowling in the cricket nets at the bottom of our garden.

Walter was joined by Aylett & Co's first employee, a tall, gangly man from Johannesburg, Dagon Sachs. Dagon had studied engineering and was a South African touch rugby player. He had been drawn into the world of investments and was referred by a Greek associate of my father. Aylett & Co was birthed in that dining room by Walter and Dagon, who spent hours scribbling notes on whiteboards.

Not long after, Aylett & Co relocated to a 90 m^2 office in Mariendal House in Newlands, Cape Town, with a jaw-dropping mountain view. It was the same mountain that we saw from our house. My dad loved that mountain, and he woke up every morning and told us he drew energy from the mountain. I watched the company develop into an award-winning investment company that applied Buffet's wisdom to its ethos and investment philosophy.

It is a Greek tradition to have the priest come to bless your house or business premises. The priest was duly invited to the new Aylett & Co office to perform the blessing ritual. This involved the priest swinging the incense burner (thymiato) while chanting as the mystifying smoke filled the office. My brothers and I were fascinated, especially when the smoke alarm was activated, and all hell broke loose. Mayhem ensued with astonished security guards rushing around, the shrill alarm sounding, and my parents reassuring everyone that all was well. In all this time, the Greek priest stuck to his guns, chanting blessings, and swinging the incense burner, not once distracted by the fuss around him.

This set a good omen for Aylett & Co. In all the years since, I've never seen my dad or his team lose their composure, never mind the state of the markets, the state of the country, or the state of the performance of their funds.

Aylett & Co's long-term performance track record is admirable, achieved with an impressively low-risk profile.

Funds under management have grown steadily, along with the team, but the company has remained small enough to keep its niche investing style. Aylett & Co is a company based on patience and setting its own high standards. Most of all, the team has a hell of a lot of fun doing their job. I have enjoyed seeing the company grow and fondly reflect on the "dining room" days.

While I was growing up, I would often visit my dad's office. Going to the office was exciting: you were surrounded by grown-ups, had to whisper, and there was an air of 'seriousness' when you walked in. When anyone asked me what my dad's office was like, I would say COLD!

It didn't matter how bad the weather was. The air-conditioning in the office was cold enough to freeze the balls off a brass monkey. I would always bring an extra jersey on office days. There were screens, computers, graphs and loads of numbers, and I often wondered why the numbers only turned red or green. The investment world apparently wasn't multi-colored.

I would stroll past the boardroom and see my father and Dagon meeting with the investment team or clients. I would remember seeing these two sitting in our family's dining room in 2005. From whiteboards to projectors, boy, these guys had come a long way. I did not fully comprehend exactly what my father did for a living, but I was fully attuned to his thinking, philosophies, and approach to life.

My dad is rather forthright, and I understood his mind and ground rules for life. He ran Aylett & Co the same way he ran the Aylett family. What I saw at Aylett & Co was merely an amplification of how it was at home: *close to the line is out.*

One rainy Cape Town afternoon, I went to my dad's office. I had taken four wickets in a cricket match earlier that day, but my teammates and coach were disappointed that I did not strike the five-wicket haul. Fittingly, my dad gave me one of his Buffett lines. *Have your own standards, my boy, do not rate your performance by the standards of others.*

Near the end of the business day, just before our au pair picked me up, I heard animated chatter in the boardroom. One of the analysts had underperformed compared to some market benchmarks and was receiving consolation from my dad. You can guess what line he gave his analyst. I shot a quick glance at the analyst and felt a strange feeling. I had no idea what the problem being discussed inside the boardroom was, but the solution to that problem made entire sense to me.

Different problems, same solutions. Keep your own scorecard in life.

When asked about what my father did for a living, my answers include: *He looks after people's money and helps people get rich or watches money grow. Oh, and let's not forget, He talks about and refers to a guy called Warren Buffet rather a lot.*

I often went off on a tangent with people about Warren Buffett and how excited I would get for my dad to return from his annual Omaha trip with a case full of See's Candies. I loved to explain how Buffett and Munger fitted into the daily life of Aylett & Co and the Aylett family. My dad never told us that much of his advice came directly from the folksy wisdom and investment principles of Warren Buffett and Charlie Munger.

I would be reading an article or listening to an interview with Warren or Charlie, hear a quote, and it would suddenly click.

The answer that Warren had just given a CNBC news reporter regarding Berkshire's decision not to invest in a particular stock was the same answer my dad had given me when asked why it wasn't a good idea to chase a fickle girl I was interested in. *We don't invest in things we don't understand, my boy.*

Funnily enough, this moment of truth regarding the source of my dad's "wisdom war chest" has occurred countless times in writing this book.

Aylett & Co had a unique feel to it, and I felt a sweet connection to the company. I gradually started to grapple with the language of investments and the company's line of business. I struggled tremendously to understand the terminology and the overall investment world. I felt I was a disappointment to my father and would ruin the perfect succession plan. During my undergraduate degree at Stellenbosch University, I took investment subjects not because I wanted to become an investor but to help me at least explain what my father did in a casual fashion without looking uncomfortable.

While writing this book, it struck me that I may not have learned how to become a talented investor like my dad but had learned pearls of life wisdom that you just don't get taught at school or university.

Without realizing it, over the years, Aylett & Co, Walter, Warren and Charlie were equipping me with valuable life lessons and teaching me how to think smartly.

'Bring your parents to school day' was rather eventful, and I would often be anxious to see if other kids in the class would even understand my dad's line of work. My dad worked with numbers and screens while other parents were doctors, architects, or held jobs that nine-year-olds could sort of understand.

To my father's credit, he would stand in front of the class and explain his job in a simple, understandable way, leaving us feeling inspired. My dad concluded his little presentation by imparting some Buffett wisdom to a group of seven-year-olds. He made eye contact with every young boy in the room as he began the famous line. "You are truly lucky in life to find the right heroes. Find a great hero and learn as much as you can about what makes them successful." My friend, Justin, cheekily chirped. "So, who's your hero, Mr. Aylett?"

Walter outside the Aylett & Co offices in Newlands, 2022.

CHAPTER 3 – HEROES

- Heroes -

"You are lucky in life if you have the right heroes".
– Warren Buffett.

My dad once told me that if I told him who my heroes were, he would have some idea of how I would turn out to be. As a kid, I associated the word 'hero' with a powerful figure sporting a silky cape, luscious long hair, and having a superpower. I pondered the definition of a hero: was it like a role model or mentor?

I constantly searched for the right type of hero to tick the boxes. A hero that, if shown to my dad, would result in me being told that I would turn out well and be successful. Like most things in life, you cannot force or chase things; they will naturally find their way to you if they are meant to be.

I was, and still am, tennis obsessed. My maternal grandmother was a first-team club tennis player, followed by my mother, who was introduced to tennis in vitro. My granny made the tennis club championship Women's Singles Final six months pregnant with my mom, and she went on to win the match in a grueling three-setter.

I guess from that point on, the gene expression was determined. As a kid, I played all sports, but it was the racket that remained in my hand. Tennis was not just a sport I competed in or played over the weekend with friends. Tennis was my life, and I ate, slept, and lived it.

In 2012, my life became extremely dark, scary, and lonely. I was 15 years old, with zero confidence. I was fearful and withdrew from my peer group. I was deep in adolescent angst and crisis. Vulnerable and desperate, I had to find a way out of this terrible darkness. Routes of escape can become dangerously perilous. Fortunately, I chose tennis.

There was a character in the tennis world that would become the cornerstone on which I created my foundation of support through this tough time. Some may say he is the best player to walk the court or has the game's most brutal yet blissful backhand. Regardless of his fame, records, and fan base, on and off the court, he helped me get through many dark times.

His name is Roger Federer. He is my hero. Watching, practicing and playing tennis, I had found an escape.

I would wake up with a heavy weight of depression on my chest. Knowing Roger was playing that evening or that I had a training session or tennis tournament to prepare for, got me to pick up that lead ball when every bone in my body told me No!

The day my mom and I snuck into a press conference at the Green Point athletics stadium. I was the last "Netherlands Donor" to grab a photo with Roger & Rafael in 2020. That same day we watched the two battle it out in doubles with Bill Gates & Trevor Noah. The event was attended by 51,954 people (the highest attendance ever recorded at a tennis match), and more than $3.5 million was raised to aid children's education in Africa.

I used Roger Federer and tennis as topics for school orals, assignments, or speeches on several occasions. Years later, in 2019, I enrolled in an event in Cape Town called *Pecha Kucha (chit-chat in Japanese)*. Based on visual storytelling, the event includes ten speakers who may use twenty slides of 20 seconds each and are given 400 seconds to tell their story. *Pecha Kucha* started in Japan in 2003 and has become a global community with chapters in over 1,200 cities.

The event happens every few months in Cape Town, with around 500 attendees. Tickets always sell out, and the organizers promote the line-up of speakers and their chosen topics well in advance.

At my first *Pecha Kucha* event, the host concluded with an invitation for people to apply to be a speaker for the next event. My father chuckled beside me and said, "You would definitely talk about old Roger, hey?"

Challenge accepted!

When preparing for this talk, I knew I could not merely go on about Roger this and Wimbledon that. I would sound like the standard fanboy. It was different for me: winning or losing, the spin-off from following my hero over the years, was unreal. It was not his record-breaking statistics or immaculate backhand that ignited the connection.

It was his tenacity, integrity, personal drive, self-belief, and resilience. Manifestly, by following my hero, certain habits had crept into my DNA, powering my success, reforming my vision, and showing me the way. I was able to hit the ball over life's net. I feared no one and respected everyone.

It dawned on me that I had found the angle and topic for my Pecha Kucha speech. Yet again, Kimon, now 23, had been guided by a Buffett principle in establishing the topic for his Pecha Kucha presentation. *'Heroes: one is truly lucky in life to find the right heroes'*

My Pecha Kucha Talk. Heroes: One is truly lucky in life to find the right heroes, 2019.

- Heroes -

My Pecha Kucha presentation opened with slides of Buffett and one of his heroes, the father of value investing and Buffett's professor at Colombia Business School, Benjamin Graham. A 19-year-old Buffett would be introduced to Benjamin Graham through Graham's book, *The Intelligent Investor*. According to Buffett, this book is by far the best book on investing ever written. After reading it, Buffett enrolled at Columbia Business School to study under Graham, with whom he developed a lifelong friendship. He later worked for Graham at his investment company, the Graham-Newman Corporation.

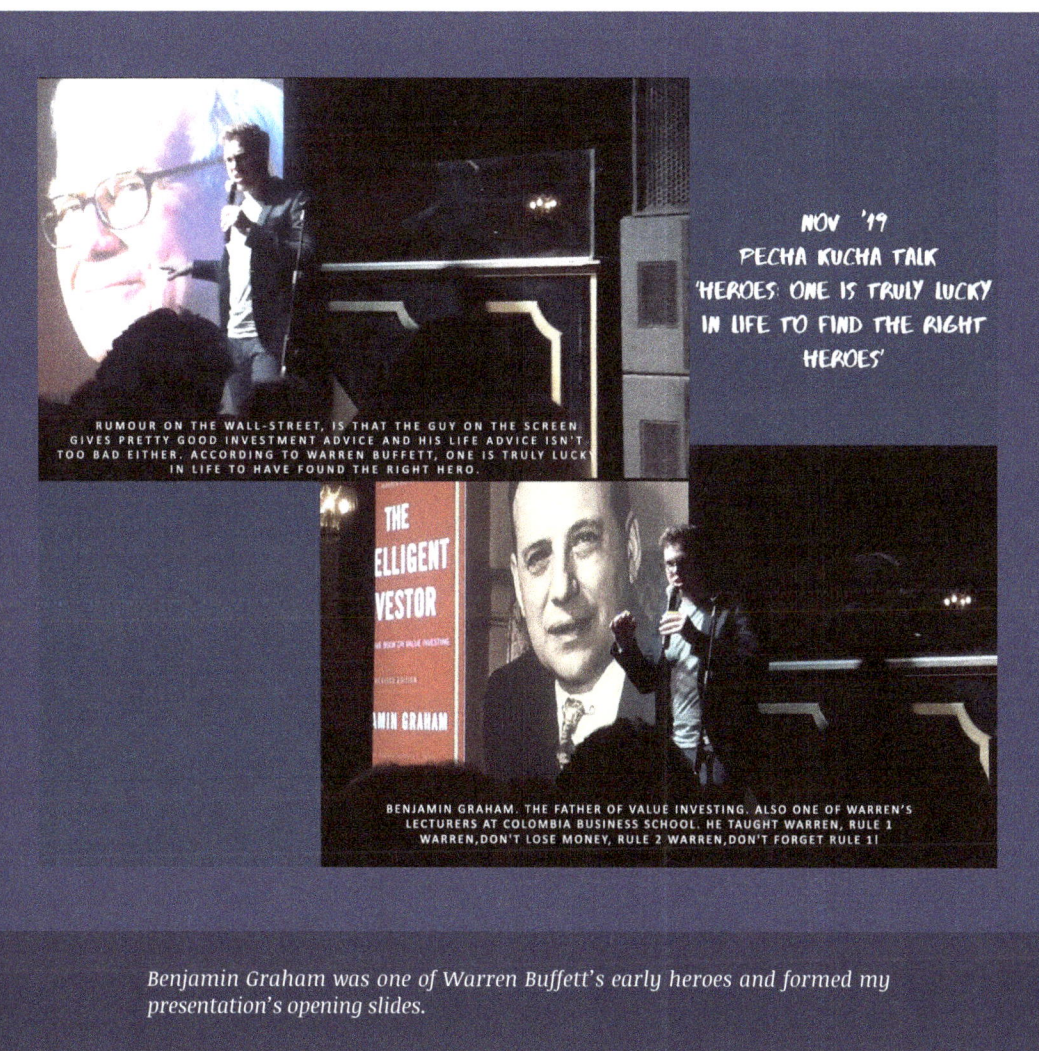

Benjamin Graham was one of Warren Buffett's early heroes and formed my presentation's opening slides.

Graham set the 19-year-old Buffett on a course that would shape his professional career. He gave Buffett the tools to explore the market's many possibilities and did it in a way that fitted Buffett's manner. In Graham's lecture room, Buffett would hear Graham's famous rule about investing, *Rule 1: Never lose money. Rule 2: Never forget rule 1.*

Graham thought Buffett was the cream among his disciples and recognized their similarity. One day, as they were going to lunch at a delicatessen near the office, Graham said, "Money won't make a difference to you and me, Warren. We'll be the same, and our wives will live better." Alongside Graham, Howard Buffett, Warren's father, would be in Warren's hero set. Howard had a huge influence on his son while he was growing up. Steeled by the examples of Graham's character, Buffett would be able to work with his trademark self-reliance and the "sweetness" of Emersonian independence, which his father had told him about. *The great man is he who in the midst of the crowd, keeps with perfect sweetness the independence of solitude* (Lowenstein, 1997:23).

Warren's late wife, Susie Buffett, has also been recognized as one of his heroes. Susie taught him a tremendous amount. From the HBO documentary 'Becoming Warren Buffett', and an article published in the online version of the New Zealand Herald, we can glean the following about Susie Buffett from her husband. *Susie really put me together; she believed in me. I would not only have not turned out to be the person I turned out to be, but I actually wouldn't have been as successful in business without that. She made me more of a whole person over the years; I've got a better understanding of human nature.*

One can learn much by observing. Warren observed Ben, Howard, and Susie. He often goes into depth about how extraordinarily lucky he has been to find heroes who have not let him down, and having these types of heroes took him a long way. Buffett goes on to explain how he went through some pretty tough and dark times but that having the right heroes helped him to overcome difficulty.

Let's circle back to that question my classmate, Justin, asked my father regarding who my father's hero was. My other buddy, Johnnie, the class clown, threw in an additional comment, *Well, it's got to be this Warren Buffett fella! He's all you talk about!* Johnnie pronounced Warren's surname as 'Buffay', and the whole class immediately thought of food assortments. Chuckling, my father smiled. He calmly stated, "Yes, Warren is up there in my heroes list, and I regard him as a role model on both a business and personal level, but he's not my go-to hero."

Who's your go-to hero, then? Johnnie blurted out.

My dad replied with a gleam in his eye, *Charlie, Charlie Munger.*

• • • • • • • • • • • •

- Charlie -

"There was only one partner who fits my bill of particulars in everyway – Charlie." - Warren Buffett.

It was a late April Sunday, approaching Camps Bay, one of the most beautiful areas along Cape Town's Atlantic Seaboard. Winter was slowly approaching, and the sunset was breathtaking, its beauty offset by a gale-force wind, something Camps Bay is famous for. My father was upstairs packing for his annual business trip to the United States; I was building Lego in the playroom with my brother, Nikos. Our little brother, Dinos, watched some cartoon series in our family room while Mom was fixing supper. Everyone was doing their own thing, rounding off the weekend.

Suddenly, Dinos came bounding into the kitchen, yelling, *Mom! Dad! Come to the family room now; you must come to see who's on TV!*

By now, the whole family, including our two dogs, were alerted. We all scurried to the family room, curious to discover who had captured his attention on the television. Rather unexpectedly, the CNBC business channel was showing, not Dinos' favorite cartoon channel.

An interview was taking place. *For those of you who have just tuned in, we have the pleasure tonight of talking with Charlie Munger, Vice-Chairman at Berkshire Hathaway and right-hand man to the Oracle of Omaha, Warren Buffett!*

We all looked at Dinos, impressed that he had recognized the name 'Charlie Munger' and had called us, but that didn't seem to be the reasoning behind the gathering in the family room. He began to explain. "You see!"

"Exactly what are we supposed to be seeing, darling?" my mom asked.

"That old man on the TV ... he's stolen our dog's name!" blustered Dinos.

Here was Walter Aylett's son triumphantly calling one of the greatest investors of all time, the man most scathing toward Wall Street who had compared bankers to heroin addicts, and let's not forget, my dad's hero, a thief?

Our beloved Beagle, Nikos's dog, was named after Charlie Munger in 2002.

- Charlie -

Never mind the 80-odd-year age difference between Munger the man and Munger the Beagle, in young Dinos' mind, the cart most certainly came before the horse in this case. It became folklore in our family that once upon a time, there was a famous man called Charlie, named after our dog, Munger. Years later, Munger's 'namesake' is going strong at age 98, while his canine counterpart is no doubt smiling indulgently down upon him from doggie heaven.

As I began to understand more about Warren Buffett, I began to understand my dad better, and I started to realize that there was indeed a figure who had had a distinct influence on both men. It was strange: I knew about Warren Buffett, having heard his name countless times as far back as I could remember; I had heard him speak on TV, and above all, everything in our household was Buffett this and Buffett that.

What I didn't know was who this so-called Charlie guy was. Supposedly Buffett's right-hand man, this was an individual who outweighed Warren Buffett on my father's heroes list and who had particularly large-looking eyes magnified by his "Coke bottle" glasses. More about Charlie's eyesight later.

Charlie was not only Buffett's business partner and close friend; in today's terms, Charlie and Warren have shared a decades-long 'bromance'. Well known for his sharp wit and pithy one-liners, Buffett has often referred to Charlie as the abominable no-man. Funnily enough, while writing this book, I discovered that what I had always thought of as Buffett one-liners were actually Charlie one-liners, thanks to my dad's frequent lack of full disclosure!

One might argue that since Charlie has influenced my father more, I should rather be writing a book, perhaps called 'The Power of No, according to Charlie Munger'.

I asked my father about this, receiving a curt answer, "If you're asking a question like that, you clearly don't know the most important characteristic of Charlie Munger."

Charlie does not like to be the center of attention and prefers to let Warren be the frontman. Okay, that answers why Warren has the lead role in this book!

While Warren Buffett is arguably one of the most admired and famous investors to have walked Wall Street, Charlie Munger has purposefully sidestepped the limelight, preferring relative anonymity instead. Other than naming our beloved Beagle after him, Munger's worldly wisdom often crept into chats with my dad. Following suit with Charlie's 'under the radar' nature, my father would not flaunt Charlie's one-liners, and he would rather use them in specific, personal situations with people close to him. Often, when sounding my dad out on something important, I would get the response from my dad, "What would Charlie do?" or "Think like Charlie."

If you receive a Charlie one-liner or principle from my father, you are in his circle of trust. He uses Warren's one-liners more readily at work, in presentations, in his written investment reports, and socially. Charlie's pearls of wisdom are reserved for more intimate conversations. Besides, when one mostly quotes Charlie Munger to the average individual, they respond with, *Charlie, who?* Friends of mine often thought my dad had lost his mind by referring to our Beagle when overhearing him delivering life advice to me, "My boy, you should know by now Munger's opinion of Wall Street bankers. They are uncontrollable, like heroin addicts." Eyes would move to our Beagle. *What on earth was 'Munger' saying to Kimon's dad?*

This Wall Street comparison certainly burst my bubble after seeing *The Wolf of Wall Street* based on the true story of Jordan Belfort, charting his sensational rise to becoming a wealthy stockbroker caught up in the high life to his demise involving crime, corruption, and the federal government. Enchanted by Leonardo DiCaprio's performance, the life of Wall Street seemed a place of magnificent thrills to me. Needless to say, my dad cut me right down on that one.

The way people describe Charlie is sometimes how I describe my dad. They are both rather blunt, enjoy giving sermons on their soapboxes, and believe that their answer is right or is the most logical or rational view. This is all relative, of course, and the reality is that their answers aren't necessarily always right for every situation. They are, however, backed up with volumes of knowledge and countless hours spent reading. My father also backed this up by saying that Charlie could get away with being a know-it-all because he is such a genius. I, too, believe my dad is part genius in his own way, and hopefully, the world will forgive him for his strong views!

I was and still am wary when in conversations with my father. I often leave the conversation low in confidence or self-esteem or feel plain stupid. It takes a thick skin, a strong sense of self, and an open mind to take what people like my father and Charlie say with a pinch of salt. Both have very high standards.

The following is from *Poor Charlie's Almanack.*

Charlie is famously known to be a disciple of Benjamin Franklin, an American polymath and one of the Founding Fathers of the United States. From 1733 to 1758, Benjamin Franklin dispensed useful and timeless advice. Among the virtues he prescribed were thrift, duty, hard work, and simplicity. Subsequently, during the following two centuries, Franklin's thoughts on these subjects were regarded as the last word. That is until a gentleman named Charlie Munger stepped forth.

Initially merely a disciple of Franklin, Charlie was soon breaking new ground. What Franklin recommended, Charlie demanded. If Franklin suggested saving pennies, Charlie raised the stakes. If Franklin said to be prompt, Charlie said to be early. Life under Franklin's rules began to look positively cushy compared with the rigor demanded by Munger (2006, 8).

Above all, Franklin possessed a quick and willing mind that enabled him to easily master each new field of endeavor he chose to undertake. It is not surprising that Charlie Munger considers Franklin his paramount hero; for Munger is largely self-taught and shares many of Franklin's distinctive characteristics (2006, 67).

I felt as if I was Benjamin Franklin and my dad was Charlie Munger, in the sense that his standards were consistently testing my own. Munger often bemoans how his professors failed to prepare him or mention the predictable patterns of obvious and extreme irrationality in the business world.

He felt that professors didn't teach students the appropriate multidisciplinary approaches by practicing over-reliance on their own models and largely ignoring important models in other disciplines.

Munger strongly believes in the multidisciplinary approach, which is his self-developed model for clear and simple thinking, yet his concepts and models are anything but simplistic. However, Charlie's thinking stands the test of time.

Charlie's observations and conclusions are based on fundamental human nature, basic truths, and core principles from a wide range of disciplines (2006, 12).

During his lifetime, Munger taught himself to be a grand master of preparation, patience, discipline, and objectivity. He has used these attributes to succeed in his personal and business endeavors, especially in his investing. With Munger's exceptional investing record in mind, equaled by Buffett's brilliance, I often asked my father why others do not routinely emulate their investment practices.

My dad would explain that the multidisciplinary approach is simply too hard for people to adopt consistently. Most importantly, few investors share Charlie and Warren's willingness to appear foolish by not following "the herd." With rigid objectivity, Charlie was content to swim against the tide of popular opinion indefinitely, if necessary. This trait I often see in my dad, trusting his own judgment even when it runs counter to the wisdom of the herd, which earned him the name many years ago in the investment industry of the 'maverick investor'. Similarly, my dad has always encouraged me to avoid herd mentality and to be an independent thinker.

Growing up, my dad quoted Charlie Munger often in the context of some family discussion. My brothers and I grew so accustomed to this that Charlie Munger seemed like a familiar, old uncle to us.

From a young age, I was fascinated by the question that asked how I could become happy, and I was perplexed about why certain people were unhappy. For a long time, I was convinced that the secret to happiness was to get a girlfriend and to be rich. I got annoyed when people said that money can't buy happiness, and I would produce some smartass comeback like, "Wouldn't you rather cry in a Lamborghini than in a VW Beetle?"

I struggled to understand how lots of money could fail to make my life happier. I got the point that money alone can't guarantee happiness, but surely having money makes it much easier to live a happier life by allowing freedom of choice. In my quest to find out how to be happy, I turned to my dad.

I assumed his answers would follow the lines of *love what you do. Spend time with friends who care about you*, and so forth. Something tangible and specific. I had an inkling that his answer might be Charlie or Warren inspired, and boy, was I right!

My boy, I can't tell you how to be happy, but I can tell you how you can guarantee misery in your life. The most important thing by far is not to resent and envy. These were things I learned from Munger, as well as not to take chemicals and never to be unreliable or late. Those few principles have taught me so much about life. Every time I hit a wall or feel depressed and find myself in a tough place, I try to avoid feeling sorry for myself. Taking chemicals, envying others, and being resentful, you'll end up miserable by doing any of these three things, I guarantee - Walter Aylett.

I was about seven when I first heard these words of wisdom. Sure enough, my dad had got them from Charlie Munger. I wasn't sure what chemicals he was referring to, but I got the idea that my dad's 'list' led to unhappiness. Okay, so now I had the answer to unhappiness. Yet I was more concerned about the opposite, finding the answer to reaching a state of happiness. Not satisfied, I went back to my dad, demanding more answers.

Okay, my boy, now that you've heard my most important Charlie line, here's the follow up one. You asked me how to be happy? I gave you a way to be unhappy. So, how can you take what I've shared with you and answer your original question?

Dad, I'm confused.

Invert, my boy, always invert! Invert, Invert, Invert. Invert the way you look at things. Turn them and the assumptions upside down. Then look again.

Great, my dad was bringing math into the answer.

- Charlie -

Inversion, my boy. Invert, always invert.

I would hear this advice repeated time and time again from my dad and would later discover that my dad unsurprisingly got this from Charlie Munger, who got it from the great German mathematician Carl Gustav Jakob Jacobi. Jacobi was known for solving difficult problems by following the man muss immer umkehren strategy or, loosely translated, 'invert, always invert'.

He believed one of the best ways to clear your thinking was to restate math problems in inverse form. By writing down the opposite of the problem he was trying to solve, he found that the solution often came to him more easily.

Inversion is a powerful thinking tool because it highlights errors and obstacles that are not always apparent at first glance. What if the opposite was true? What if I focused on a different side of this situation? Rather than asking how to do something, ask how not to do it.

Back to my dad.

So, my boy, we are essentially trying to work out what X is (answer to happiness) by turning the question backward. That is, by studying how to create non-X. If you want to be happy, write out a list of things that will result in not being happy, and then stay away from the things on that list. e.g., do drugs, be envious and resentful.

Munger has a prime inversion example as an effective way to be smart: to consistently not be dumb. The good news about this approach is that it is easier not to be dumb than to be smart since you can often simply avoid certain types of decisions and activities that are bound to show that you are not smart.

Just avoid things like racing trains to the crossing, doing cocaine, etc. Develop good mental habits. A lot of success in life and business comes from knowing what you want to avoid: early death, a bad marriage, etc. (Munger, 2006, 137).

My dad would solidify this perspective by quoting Charlie yet again. *If you know where you're going to die, simply stay away from that place.*

Many would make light of Charlie's seemingly flippant advice, but it faithfully reflects both his views and his methods for avoiding mistakes in investing. Munger is known to focus first on what to avoid and what NOT to do before considering the positive steps to take in each situation. "All I want to know is where I am going to die, so I'll never go there."

In business, as in life, Charlie gains an enormous advantage by ruling out the unfavorable parts of the chessboard – freeing his time and attention for the most fruitful areas. He strives to reduce complex situations to the most basic fundamentals, free from emotion.

As much as I would love to go into similar depth with other Munger-isms peppered throughout my upbringing, this would take up the rest of the book. As mentioned, Charlie does not like the limelight, and I'll respect that.

Perhaps some readers may wonder about the "upside down" text of the previous page, and it was simply me having fun with a literal play on the inversion quote on page 83.

Invert the way you look at things. Turn them and the assumptions upside down. Then look again.

I bet some of you thought that it was a publishing error. Maybe it changed the way you regarded this book, and perhaps it changed your perspective a little by having to turn the book upside down for a page and then upside down again; maybe it left you wondering what the hell was going on.

That's the power of inversion. Got you, didn't I?

Remember that humorous dialogue at the beginning of this book? Both scenarios exhibited resentment toward the bully to the extent that the wronged party yelled, "I wish Michael were dead!"

How many times does one encounter resentment in life? I'm talking about that school bully, an unkind boss at work, or that one person who is genuinely a horrible human being and yet seems to get away with it. They still attract the best-looking partners and are promoted to top positions. This is sure to fuel your resentment chamber as you watch their selfish life decisions while being mystified about how such a terrible person could be so 'successful' in life. The truth is that one will face many 'Michaels' in life.

During a speech to Harvard Westlake graduates, Charlie elaborated on resentment: "Life is hard enough to swallow without squeezing in the bitter rind of resentment. If you find it impossible to quit feeling resentful, go cold turkey." He suggested applying the 'Disraeli compromise' (Munger, 2006:154).

As Benjamin Disraeli rose to become the Prime Minister of the United Kingdom, he learned to give up vengeance. However, he retained an outlet for resentment by writing the names of all the people who had wronged him on a piece of paper and placing it in a drawer. Then, from time to time, he reviewed those names and took pleasure in noting how the world had taken his enemies down without his assistance.

My father would react to my resentment tantrums by giving me a piece of paper and a pencil. I didn't have to hear the Charlie quote to know what to do next.

Charlie adds a very important piece of advice for avoiding discouraging outcomes and focusing on the positive. "Avoid feeling sorry for yourself." This is often easier said than done when life hands out an unexpected backhand, and it's all too tempting to have a 'pity party'. Not only has

Munger's investment track record borne out the consistent approaches that he preaches, but his personal life has also shown how Charlie steadfastly deals with adversity.

It was a huge blow for Munger when at age 29, his marriage of eight years fell apart. According to his friends, Munger walked away with very little and resorted to living in The Pasadena Club. According to *Damn Right: Behind the Scenes with Berkshire Hathaway Billionaire Charlie Munger, the biography by Janet Lowe*, commenting on his yellow Pontiac with a terrible paint job, his daughter, Molly, asked, "Daddy, this car is just awful, a mess. Why do you drive it?" The broke Munger replied, *To discourage gold diggers.*

This testing time for Munger was to get worse. Not long after the divorce, Munger's nine-year-old son Teddy was diagnosed with leukemia (cancer of the blood cells), which sadly, at the time, had a low recovery rate. With no health insurance, Munger had to pay for everything out-of-pocket, adding further financial strain. According to his friend, Rick Guerin, Munger would walk the streets of Pasadena crying after visits to the hospital, where he would hold his young son, who was slowly dying. Teddy died a year later, in 1955.

I can't imagine any experience in life worse than losing a child inch by inch (Munger, 44)

At a 2007 speech given to graduating students at the University of Southern California Law School, Munger said, *Another thing, of course, is life will have terrible blows, horrible blows, unfair blows. Doesn't matter. And some people recover, and others don't. And here I think the attitude of Epictetus is the best. He thought that every misfortune in life was an opportunity to behave well. Every mischance in life was an opportunity to learn something and your duty was not to be submerged in self-pity but to utilize the terrible blows in a constructive fashion. That is a very good idea.*

As if Munger hadn't suffered his share of personal difficulties, in his fifties, he lost his eyesight in his left eye after a botched cataract surgery and went on to have it removed due to terrible pain. When doctors told him, he had developed a condition that could cause his remaining eye to fill up with blood and become blind, Munger, pragmatic as always, took braille lessons. Fortunately, his eye condition didn't deteriorate, and he still has sight in his right eye. The 'Coke bottle' glasses now make sense to me.

I did not truly understand the *"don't feel sorry for yourself"* quote until 2015. My experiences with the death of a loved one had been when my papou (Greek for grandfather) died unexpectedly in 2006 and when my beloved Jack Russell, Ruby, left us in 2018. Other than a few really tough breakups, those were my closest experiences with loss.

I may not have experienced losing a child inch by inch, but at the beginning of 2015, I started losing my parents inch by inch. After 27 years of marriage, my parents were divorcing.

One would assume that I applied the 'have no self-pity' rule to the pain my brothers and I were feeling, but the real lesson came in watching how my father recovered from losing his soulmate.

I was fine until my divorce happened and Charlie gave me the tools to cope ... the wisdom and the sadness that goes with divorce. I don't think I could have done it without Charlie Munger. It's crazy to say, but things like not resenting, hating other people, and not feeling sorry yourself — also, the concept of getting what you deserve. I mean, I had to ask myself: what role did I play in my divorce? And I think you can only put that down when you can answer the question: did you get what you deserved? And going forward? I think I do get what I deserve, you know, and that's Charlie. Whereas Buffett is more about focus, business decisions, he's not particularly good on life. He hasn't really influenced me in life. Other than some very good stuff like not letting words affect you or controlling your emotional reactions or not personalizing things and being kind and that sometimes you have to be ruthless in business. - Walter Aylett.

While walking the streets crying, Charlie soon realized he was the only one feeling sorry for himself. Regardless of the heartache, unfairness, and trauma of a situation like losing a child, life moves on. So too, do the people around you. Reading about how Charlie dealt with terrible blows taught my dad not to have self-pity.

Self-pity is destabilizing, stupefying, crippling, useless and foolish. Choosing to go against the grain means you're sometimes going to fail. You are more vulnerable to bouts of self-pity and despair and must work tirelessly to avoid feeling sorry for yourself.

I've personally felt that my dad is more like Charlie than Warren, and they both excel at telling others what they think they should know. This trait can often cause antipathy to the extent that it is sometimes annoying, which can be partially counteracted by being more empathetic.

While some might see this trait as a social deficiency, I agree with the great Cicero, who described it as a helpful virtue easing the process of instructing the world.

As a parting shot, let's look at what Warren has to say. This sets us up well for the next chapter.

Look first for someone both smarter and wiser than you are. After locating him (or her), ask him or her not to flaunt their superiority so that you may enjoy acclaim for the many accomplishments that sprang from their thoughts and advice. Seek a partner who will never second-guess you nor sulk when you make expensive mistakes. Look for a generous person who will put up their own money and work for peanuts. Finally, join with someone who will constantly add to the fun as you travel a long road together.

In Franklin's famous essay, he says that an older mistress makes sense, and he goes on to give eight very good reasons as to why this is so. His clincher: 'And lastly, they are so grateful.'

Charlie and I have been partners for 45 years. I'm not sure whether he had seven other reasons for selecting me. But I definitely meet Ben's eight criteria. I couldn't be more grateful (Buffett, 2006:1).

∙ ∙ ∙ ∙ ∙ ∙ ∙ ∙ ∙ ∙ ∙ ∙

CHAPTER 5 – CHOOSING THE RIGHT PARTNER

"You want to associate with people who are the kind of person you'd like to be. You'll move in that direction. And the most important person by far in that respect is your spouse. I can't overemphasize how important that is."
– Warren Buffett.

I think my chapter would be about partnerships, about different skills and strengths people bring to their partnerships. I think one of the reasons Berkshire Hathaway's such a success is because of the nature of the partnership. I think that sort of partnership is a huge advantage for any business. I think you've seen the same sort of things that have to do with Rand Merchant Bank, a leading African corporate and investment bank, where there were basically three partners who had different skills, different strengths, and they built a highly successful business. I think that's it for me. If I tried one chapter, I would focus on the partnership. What it's brought to the party. – Piet Viljoen, Executive Director and Portfolio Manager of Counterpoint Asset Manager.

How did Warren and Charlie initially cross paths? The story is told by the pair with obvious enjoyment to Becky Quick in the fantastic CNBC interview 'Buffett & Munger: A Wealth of Wisdom,' aired in June 2021. In the late 1950s, Buffett was asked to come and see Dorothy Davis and her husband, Eddie Davis, a prominent doctor in Omaha. They were interested in hearing about his investing.

By his own admission, the young Buffett was quite full of himself and couldn't talk fast enough about stocks. Dorothy Davis listened intently while her husband sat in the corner, seemingly not paying much attention. After a while, Dr. Davis said to his wife, "I'm going to give him $100,000 to invest." With only $500,000 under management, this was still a lot of money for Buffett. When he asked the doctor why he was giving him $100,000 to invest, he answered, "You remind me of Charlie Munger." Buffett's cheeky answer was, "Well, I don't know who Charlie Munger is, but I like him!"

Charlie was like a son to the Davis couple. His dad was best friends with Eddie Davis, and his mom was best friends with Dorothy Davis, and they clearly loved him.

In 1959, Charlie visited Omaha from Los Angeles when his dad died, and the Davis's arranged a dinner for the two to meet. Warren recalls that five minutes in, Charlie was sort of rolling on the floor, laughing at his own jokes, which is exactly what he would do. It struck him that he wouldn't find anyone like this, and the two just hit it off.

We can learn more about the start of the friendship in Warren Buffett: *The Making of an American Capitalist* (88, 1997). Warren and Charlie had a lot in common, and both grew up in Omaha and, as youngsters, had worked at Ernest Buffett's grocery store, Warren's grandfather.

They both agree that what they learned from working at the grocery store was they didn't want to work at a grocery store!

Soon after their first meeting, they met again at Dick Holland's, a mutual friend, and talked non-stop. Munger, apparently clutching one drink all evening, was so intent on holding the floor that as he lifted his glass and tilted his head to swallow, he would raise the other hand in a stop sign so no one would butt in! (Lowenstein, 1997:88).

Their friendship developed further over the summer holidays when the Buffett's went to California and visited the Munger's. Buffett was often sprawled on the floor when he was home, cradling the phone and talking to Charlie. Little Susie Buffett said a familiar lament at dinner time, "Oh-oh, Dad's talking to Charlie." She recalled, "They talked for hours. They anticipated each other. It was like they hardly had to say anything. It was … 'Yeah-Uh-huh-I know what you mean … right'." (Lowenstein, 1997:88).

Buffett said he and Munger thought so much alike it was 'spooky.' Unlike many of Buffett's friends, Munger was not in awe of him, which must have strengthened the friendship. Buffett urged Munger to switch careers and become an investor, and he kept telling Charlie that practicing law was a waste of his talent. Fortunately, Munger didn't disagree!

At the time, Munger was a real estate attorney at *Munger, Tolles & Olson LLP*, and as he says, Buffett scorned what he did for a living. He eventually wised up to Buffett's advice, realizing that he would always be charging by the hour as a lawyer. This limitation of a capped income certainly wasn't first prize, and as his friend, Warren, repeatedly told him, "There are better ways to make a living." From a young age, his primary motivation for increasing wealth was freedom, and a change was required.

Munger gave up the law practice in Los Angeles to do what Buffett was doing in Omaha. The two had a lot of fun in those early days, with Charlie describing it as a hunting expedition. In 1965, Buffett had bought enough shares in a textile business to take ownership of the floundering company. Little did he know then that the company, Berkshire Hathaway, would become one of the world's biggest holding companies. In a 2010 interview, Buffett said that acquiring Berkshire Hathaway was his worst trade ever. He realized he had invested a lot of money in a terrible business. Be that as it may, Berkshire Hathaway was to become the foundation for everything the savvy investor has done since.

In 1967, a good insurance company came along; he bought it for Berkshire Hathaway, although in hindsight, Buffett acknowledges that he should have put the investment into an entirely new company. The textile-heavy Berkshire Hathaway would continue to be a deadweight for Buffett for twenty years until he eventually gave up on it. At first, the company was made up purely of textile assets, but over time Buffett built more things into it *(Buffett and Munger a Wealth of Wisdom*, YouTube, 2021).

From that first insurance company deal, Warren was soon joined by Charlie Munger, who steadily invested in undervalued companies. Learning from their mistakes was common for them, and one notable instant was their early joint investment in Blue Chip Stamps. Munger recounts that all the businesses they owned together during the early days disappeared. Buffett jokingly says that's because they failed, which Munger qualifies by saying that they took so much out of them before they failed that it still worked out well for them (*Buffett and Munger a Wealth of Wisdom*, YouTube, 2021).

Buffett and Munger's perspectives on life have much to do with their shared upbringing in Omaha, with its deep Midwestern values. A cornerstone for both men has been the influence of being surrounded by good people starting from their parents, their parent's friends, and the good folk from Omaha. Buffett refers to both he and Munger always seeking out the company of older people, even from a young age. Ruefully Warren concedes that they're starting to run low on this constituency at their age. Charlie jokes that he acted like he was 100 years old, even when he was young. One might say that this extraordinary pair were both born old souls.

Until 1978, the quirky pair worked together informally. Following a major market drop, Charlie's investment firm in Los Angeles suffered severe losses. Charlie, confident that the market would recover, had no time to deal with silly clients calling non-stop. He closed the investment firm, and yes, you guessed right. Charlie jumped ship and invested in Berkshire, receiving shares in return.

Now that Charlie was a shareholder in Berkshire, a whole new chapter together awaited them. Charlie Munger became Berkshire Hathaway's Vice-Chairman, cementing his role as Warren's business partner. Together, the two were lethal. Warren's investment style, influenced by Benjamin Graham, was to invest in terrific bargains until Charlie came along.

If it's worth $1, you pay 10 cents. Charlie convinced Warren to consider quality; to invest in terrific businesses. By investing and paying for quality, hallmark investments such as *See's Candies* and *Coca-Cola*, made by Berkshire Hathaway, are prime examples of companies whose primary value would be earned in the future. The candy business has produced a steady stream of capital that Berkshire Hathaway has used to invest in other attractive companies and arguably has been their 'sweetest' investment holding. I know, I know; I just couldn't help myself.

Damn Right: Behind the Scenes with Berkshire Hathaway Billionaire Charlie Munger (Lowe, 2003:110) reveals that Charlie is a tough taskmaster. Warren quickly grew accustomed to his tough stance on potential investments, calling him the 'abominable' no-man, with answers ranging from "yes" and "no" to "too tough to understand." The pair are said never to have argued, each seemingly entirely comfortable in what they do. Warren's role is to allocate capital and keep managers enthusiastic, and he uses Charlie as the ultimate litmus test. If Charlie can't think of a reason not to do something, it gets the green light.

A partner, ideally, is capable of working alone. You can be a dominant partner, a subordinate partner, or an always collaborative equal partner. I've done all three [...] People couldn't believe that I suddenly made myself a subordinate partner to Warren. But there are some people who are okay to be a subordinate partner to. I didn't have the kind of ego that prevented it. There are always people who will be better at something than you are. You have to learn to be a follower before you can become a leader. People should learn to play all roles. You can divide things up in different ways (Munger, 2006:23).

Since Dr. Eddy Davis linked Warren Buffett to Charlie Munger, the similarity between the two has often been observed. One of Warren's strengths is that he is good at saying no, but Charlie is simply better at it. Howard Buffett, Warren's eldest son, has been quoted as considering his father the second smartest person he's ever known, and Charlie takes the honors. For obvious reasons and to keep the family peace, there is no official record of Howard's sentiment (Lowe 2006:50).

While Charlie may be perceived as being negative, his ability to think differently allows him to reach independent, potentially unexpected conclusions from which to make good decisions. Despite Charlie's apparent negativity, he and Warren tend to think alike, which can be dangerous. If a mistake goes through one filter, it will likely go through the other (Lowe, 2006:504).

Damn Right: Behind the Scenes with Berkshire Hathaway Billionaire Charlie Munger (110, 2003) illustrates how the unique relationship between Munger and Buffett is far more than simply a business arrangement; it is deeply personal.

Warren has this to say about Charlie. "Though Charlie can be self-willed, preoccupied, and abrupt, he's just the best pal a guy could have."

The Greek philosopher and scientist Aristotle was born in Macedonia in 384 B.C. and is still regarded as one of the greatest thinkers of all time. "Wishing to be friends is quick work, but friendship is a slow-ripening fruit" is attributed to this towering figure from ancient Greece (Tang, 2018).

Aristotle identified three types of *philia* (friendship); **friendships of utility, friendships of pleasure, and friendships of the good.**

Friendships of utility are those mainly due to the benefits each person brings to the table, such as being business partners.

Friendships of pleasure are those where people click because of the enjoyment it offers, like friends hanging out over shared interests and hobbies.

Friendships of the good, the most important type, are also the hardest to find. These friends respect one another, they appreciate each other's qualities, and they want to aid and assist the other person because they recognize their greatness. These friendships often last for many years (Tang, 2018).

When one looks at the friendship between Warren and Charlie, spanning over 60 years, what makes it even more remarkable is that it reflects not one but all three of Aristotle's types of friendship. They are business partners; they get huge pleasure from one another's company and share tremendous respect and appreciation for one another.

One might argue that their rich friendship has contributed more value to each other's lives than all the billions of dollars these two have acquired. It certainly sets the bar high as far as friendships go.

Did Warren Buffett get lucky by meeting Charlie Munger and going on to create one of the most successful business partnerships of all time? In *The Warren Buffett CEO: Secrets from the Berkshire Hathaway Managers* by author Robert P. Miles, Barry Tatelman of Jordan's Furniture has this to say about Buffett.

I think a lot of people talk about Warren as being this great businessman, which of course, he is, but I think Warren's greatest asset is the way he analyzes people, the way he sizes them up. He can tell when he meets people what they're really like. I think he likes to be involved with people that he likes and trusts, and he is a great judge of character. I'm not saying that because he picked us, but because he's picked a lot of great people over the years.

Perhaps luck had less to do with Warren's choice of a business partner than his talent for recognizing a like-minded individual.

In the book *The Snowball: Warren Buffett and the Business of Life*, Warren offered this sage career advice:

People ask me where they should go to work, and I always tell them to go to work for those they admire the most. It's crazy to take little in-between jobs just because they look good on your résumé. That's like saving sex for old age. Do what you love and work for whom you admire the most, and you've given yourself the best chance in life you can.

Aha! Did you spot the clue to the title of this book? More on this later.

At a talk between Buffett and Bill Gates at Columbia University, New York, the audience was surprised when Warren revealed that for him, choosing the right life partner makes the biggest difference of all in your life.

You want to associate with people who are the kind of person you'd like to be. You'll move in that direction, and the most important person by far in that respect is your spouse. I can't overemphasize how important that is.

Marry the right person. I'm serious about that. It will make more difference in your life than anything else. It will change your aspirations, all kinds of things (cnbc.com, 2018).

Warren Buffett: The Making of an American Capitalist (84) reveals more about the relationship between Warren and his first wife, Susie Buffett. Warren's face would light up when Susie entered the room. She would run her fingers through his hair, fix his tie, sit on his lap, hug him. She sustained him. According to Warren, *Susie removed the thorns one by one.*

Buffett claims that there were two turning points in his life.

One when I came out of the womb and one when I met Susie … (cnbc.com, 2018).

… Your marriage with someone is the most important partnership of your life. What happened with me would not have happened without her. Susie ultimately put me together. She helped me grow up. She was one of my greatest teachers (Warren Buffett in Becoming Warren Buffett, 2017).

In the 2017 HBO documentary "Becoming Warren Buffett," the billionaire investor credits some of his greatest qualities to his first wife, Susan. *I just got very, very, very lucky. I was a lopsided person, and it took a while, but she just stood there with a little watering can and just nourished me along and changed me.*

According to the documentary, although they never divorced, Susan moved away from Omaha in 1977. The two remained very close, and Susie helped to orchestrate Buffett's relationship with Astrid Menks. After Susan Buffett's death, Warren and Astrid married on August 30, 2006, on his 76th birthday, in an intimate and private ceremony.

A partner does not necessarily have to be a romantic partner; they can be a business partner or a good friend who simply has your back in life. I met such a friend at university when we were both in our second year and studying for the same degree, Wesleigh.

Wes and I quickly became study buddies as well as good social friends. He was remarkably different from me, and we came from opposite backgrounds. He came from a modest upbringing, from a family of no-nonsense, tough survivors. By comparison, my life was far more comfortable. For instance, I had visited almost 20 countries, and Wes had rarely checked in at an airport.

Our friendship matured, and we taught one another about lifestyle, fashion, music, and women. We had different perspectives but shared a passion for business; he for investments and I for marketing. Financial Management provided some common ground.

It's important to note that Warren and Charlie's lessons were not taught at any school or university I attended, even if you were majoring in investments. Traditional economics, finance and business theories were shoved down your throat like those dreaded Friday night tequila shots. What happens the next morning? You throw up - just like on the test paper - and simply regurgitate textbook answers.

MISTEACHING INVESTING

Beta and modern portfolio theory and the like - none of it makes any sense to me. We're trying to buy businesses with sustainable competitive advantages at a low, or even a fair, price. How can professors spread this (nonsense that a stock's volatility is a measure of risk)? I've been waiting for this craziness to end for decades. It's been dented, but it's still out there … Warren once said to me, 'I'm probably misjudging academia generally in thinking so poorly of it because the people that interact with me have bonkers theories' (Munger, 2006:101).

Ten to one, when I mentioned Warren Buffett or Charlie Munger to my classmates, there was simply no common ground, perhaps other than associating their names with two old men in some faraway galaxy in America's Midwest. This was extremely odd to me. As soon as I shared with Wes how Warren Buffett and Charlie Munger fitted into the life of the Aylett family, it was as if someone was telling me that their dad was a huge tennis player and that they slavishly followed Roger Federer. At last, someone who understood!

Wes was my only friend who 'confidently' knew who Buffett and Munger were. He had read every book and article and watched every interview with Buffett and Munger. To have found a friend and a peer with limited exposure to the investment world and yet with this insight and understanding was simply incredible. With Wes, it was different. I mean, his parents were involved in construction. How the hell did this guy even know about Buffett and Munger?

Wes naturally looked up to my dad and soaked up any investment information he shared. Wes and I drifted apart academically in our final university years, but the friendship endured and grew stronger. We would spend hours chatting about Warren and Charlie, my trips to Omaha to attend the Berkshire Hathaway AGM, my father, and his asset management company. Over time, it became apparent that I did not share Wes's passion for becoming an investment analyst. There was, however, a shared passion for the wider world of investing and for two of its remarkable figures, Warren Buffett and Charlie Munger. This shared interest led to my sharing the following story with you.

Wes and I would share a private study room in the library, where we studied and indulged in 'Warren and Charlie' talk. A student was limited to four hours at a time in a study room. Wes would book from 8 a.m. to 12 p.m., and I would book from 1 p.m. to 5 p.m. Of these eight hours, I can confidently say that 30 to 40 percent involved 'Warren and Charlie' talk.

Our passion for chatting about Warren and Charlie escalated to the point that we started calling each other Warren and Charlie, him being Warren and me Charlie. Initially, it was a personal joke and would be a tease sparked during drunken chats.

To this day, I call him Warren, and he still calls me Charlie. If one of us actually uses the other person's real name, we immediately know something is wrong, or we are extremely upset with the other.

Wes has progressed tremendously in life. He was one of eighteen students to get into a postgraduate program that only accepts a handful of the top students from among 400-odd finance undergraduates. After graduating, he started working at Aylett & Company Fund Managers.

I admire Wes for his tremendous kindness, soul and most importantly his passion for the task. We don't see as much of each other as before, as he needs to balance his work life with a steady girlfriend and ultimately adjust to this next step in his life.

I suppose that if we want to call ourselves Warren and Charlie, we should have a partnership like theirs. One works in California, the other in the Midwest; they see each other several times a year and spend countless hours on the phone discussing the next move.

Often my phone will ring, and I'll pick up and hear a familiar voice. "Charlie boy, what's your take on...?"

Back to matters of the heart. The tricky part about picking the right romantic partner is truly understanding if that person and the relationship are right for you in the long run. I've given the matter a great deal of thought, having witnessed so many of my friends' parents getting a divorce or separating—even Buffett and his beloved Susie and Bill and Melinda Gates. Now I have joined that club with my own parents splitting up. How can one tell at an early stage and avoid waking up midway through your fifties, feeling compelled to break from such a long-term relationship?

I came upon a comedian whose content has provided me with profound insight into choosing the right partner. He is a 27-year-old Irishman named Daniel Sloss, who recently had a very popular Netflix special called *JIGSAW*. He also raises important questions about how we think and behave through comedy. *JIGSAW* touched on the topic of relationships, a 'love letter' to all the single people in the world. At one stage, it was claimed that the show had caused over 10,000 breakups, divorces, and canceled weddings. Whether true or not, Sloss has an interesting jigsaw puzzle analogy.

He begins by elaborating on how his generation has become obsessed with starting 'the rest of their lives' and whether they are willing to give up the one they are currently living. He shares a story that happened when he was seven years old and asked his dad about the meaning of life. His father replied with a beautiful analogy that portrayed our lives as a jigsaw puzzle. He explained how we are all piecing together our jigsaws with every lesson we learn and everything we experience. The catch is that we have all lost the box and are left to guess what the image should look like.

Like any other jigsaw puzzle, we should start piecing it from all four corners: family, friends, hobbies/interests and our job. The big question remains: What about the centerpiece of the puzzle? Sloss continues, *Well, that's the partner piece. You want this perfect person who you've never met before to come out of nowhere, fit your life perfectly, complete you, and make your life whole for the first time* (Sloss, 2018).

The analogy led him to believe that you are broken and, therefore, not whole if you are not with someone. In his show, he criticizes our society for promoting this 'perfect romance' ideology; for making children believe that every princess needs a prince and vice versa.

We mustn't forcefully 'jam' the wrong person into our jigsaw puzzle, even though they do not actually fit in. We even move other pieces around to ensure this person fits in. We would rather have something in the center of our jigsaw than feel empty and have nothing.

One must look for the same qualities in the type of 'partners' one works with as with one's soul mate. According to Buffett, Berkshire looks for three things when it hires people: intelligence, energy, and integrity. If integrity is lacking, intelligence and energy count for nothing (inc.com, 2020).

Choosing the right partner is rarely easy or straightforward. Circumstances and people change. As Buffett has portrayed in his partnership with Charlie Munger, the key to a successful partnership is, to be honest, hardworking and, most importantly, have fun together.

In business, you choose partners. In life, what happens is you fall in love with a partner. That's it. And then you deal with whatever comes your way. Now, if there's no more love, then there's no more partnership.
- Zurk Botha, a client of Aylett & Co, Owner of Zurk Botha Associates (Pty) Ltd, who has attended Berkshire seven times.

Munger and I have kept a sense of humor while building Berkshire Hathaway. It's almost hilarious, it's been so much fun. We've had so much fun in our partnership over the years. (Buffett, Lowe 2003, 8).

One can also apply these criteria to choosing friends and calculating which people are true friends. My father would give me the 'friend test' to apply when I was unsure whether someone was merely friends with me because they had a hidden agenda. I hated being used.

Back in World War 2, there were many Germans who were friends with Jews. When the Gestapo would search for Jews in hiding, it was regarded as a serious criminal offense if a fellow German was hiding a Jewish person or helping him or her to hide. If you were caught harboring a Jew, it was very likely that both of you would be killed. This was the true test of a friendship between a German and a Jew. Would your German friend hide you to save your life, thereby putting his or her own life at risk?

This 'true friend test' has stood me in good stead when choosing my friends and partners.

Asking, Will this person 'hide' me? It is a deceptively simple way to determine your true friends.

· · · · · · · · · · · ·

CHAPTER 6 – WOODSTOCK FOR CAPITALISTS

A pilgrimage is a journey, often into an unknown or foreign place, where a person goes in search of new or expanded meaning about their self, others, nature, or a higher good, through the experience. It can lead to a personal transformation, after which the pilgrim returns to their daily life
- (Wikipedia, 2020).

For many, attending a Berkshire Hathaway AGM is much like a faith-healing. Rumor has it that some people even take their spouses to the AGM for their wedding anniversary. I wonder what these people have to say about their partner's attempts at romance!

Buffett and Munger walk onto the podium each year, and the crowd settles into a reverential silence. There is a quart of Cherry Coke on the dais for Buffett, who will race through the formal business of the meeting before enthusiastically opening the floor to questions.

Hours of smart rambling ensue, covering uncut versions of annual reports and with Buffett and Munger responding to questions on Berkshire and on business in general (Lowenstein, 1997:296).

At my second AGM, I started to recognize Munger's mannerisms. Essentially Charlie plays the dour sidekick. He peppers his remarks with references to "civilization", which he seems to feel is often in peril.

He does not participate in the meeting's carnival atmosphere and is completely unaffected by the outpouring of adulation from the audience. He doesn't care whether there are five attendees or 40,000; his pompous answers remain the same (Lowenstein, 1997:296).

In comparison, Buffett soaks up the applause and admiration at Berkshire meetings. He cracks joke after joke.

As he pans the crowd, his eyebrows seem to waltz about his forehead.

His eyes reflect a true love for seeing the same faces – people he has known for years, people he has made rich beyond their wildest imagination (Lowenstein 1997:296).

Learning from Warren isn't too hard; many books about the man exist. He often gives speeches, writes articles, and isn't shy to make public appearances.

He has published lengthy annual letters to shareholders for decades. Charlie, on the other hand, is something of a dark horse, and far fewer books are written about him; he is a much less prolific writer and public speaker.

At a Berkshire AGM – besides the overall experience of networking, shopping in the exhibition hall, and hearing Warren wax lyrical about investment insights – one has the rare chance to experience Charlie's inimitable intellect.

On stage at the AGM, Warren generally takes the first stab at answering a question but then usually turns and says, *Charlie?*

Immobile and expressionless, Charlie frequently replies, *I have nothing to add.*

Those five words have become a trademark that often delights Warren and the audience. I'm convinced that Charlie secretly plays on this.

· · · · · · · · · · · · ·

They are an iconic duo. Pictured at the 2005 Berkshire Hathaway AGM.

At a special acquisition meeting in 1998, Warren mischievously showed up with a cardboard cut-out of Charlie and a recording saying, 'I have nothing to add'. Buffett used this cheeky prop half a dozen times; Warren would get this impish look each time, not bothering to hide his obvious enjoyment.

Charlie's trademark reply could suggest a grumpy public persona. While highlighting his and Warren's relationship, the partners are seamlessly attuned to one another's thoughts.

When Warren answers a question, Charlie is usually satisfied with the response and disinclined to add more (Munger, 2006:84).

On the odd occasion, Charlie does deliver a few grumbled lines. I remember a humorous example back at the 2018 Berkshire AGM. A top financial journalist had grilled a question on cryptocurrencies.

'*Cryptocurrencies will come to bad endings*', Warren replies. Then turning to his partner, '*Anything to add, Charlie?*'

Charlie grumbled and calmly stated, 'I like cryptocurrencies a lot less than you do. To me, it's just dementia.

'It's like waking up one morning, going outside, and seeing that your neighbors are trading turds, and you decide you can't be left out'.

Yup, a 96-year-old just schooled a top financial journalist by comparing trading cryptocurrencies to turds. Gotta love it!

Charlie's wisdom really shines through in a way that one can tap into. He talks about something called Lollapalooza. For example, the whole exponential company boom on the American stock market was a Lollapalooza, which really is a simple way of describing when many different forces come together and reinforce each other in one direction. He's just inspirational and more cerebral, perhaps at the AGM ...

... Of course, with the term Lollapalooza, Munger has coined the term for factors which reinforce and greatly amplify each other. It is when several models combine, you get knowledge, Lollapalooza effects. When two, three or four forces are operating in the same direction.

- Alec Hogg, South African media entrepreneur, broadcaster and writer.

At the AGM, individuals often ask the two famous investors what books they should be reading.

A special feature each year is the bookstore provided by the Bookworm, which has been servicing Omaha for over 25 years.

Only books approved by Mr. Buffett are sold at the Berkshire Hathaway AGM, covering titles by and about the company, Warren Buffett, Charlie Munger, the Berkshire managers and investing.

I wonder if *Sex Before 80!* this very book you are reading will make it onto Mr. Buffett's Berkshire Hathaway list of recommended reading!

Other than Aylett & Co's investment philosophy being based on Buffett and Munger's thinking, their portfolios hold a considerable amount of Berkshire Hathaway shares.

Clients, curious about the effect and influence that Warren and Charlie have had on the company responsible for investing their life savings, receive a simple explanation from Walter.

The reason we feel strongly at Aylett & Co about returning to Berkshire each year is ultimately to reset the compass to true North ... clear the windshield, gauge our thinking and allow clients and fellow colleagues to gain a true understanding behind the Aylett & Co way, and who inspires it.

We go there to learn, not merely investment learning but life learning. We want to become lifelong learning machines.

The crazy thing is that after 20 years of going to Berkshire, I can confidently say the story doesn't change.

Various Berkshire moments from 2012 & 2018.

May '12, outside Buffett's home, Farnam Street, Omaha, with fellow Aylett & Co analyst, Justin Ritchie.

May '18, jetlagged, tired and amped to get our seats.

06:00AM Queing outside the CHI health center 2012.

It has become a tradition for Aylett & Co to make the annual pilgrimage to Omaha, and these Berkshire visits are integral to how things are done at the company. My dad starts planning his next Omaha trip almost as soon as he's returned from the Berkshire AGM. Omaha is similar to Bloemfontein, a city in South Africa with a population of around 500,000, situated in a flat area and has produced some pretty impressive names. Omaha has Warren Buffett, Andy Roddick, Malcolm X and Sting. Bloemfontein has borne countless sports stars, JRR Tolkien, The Lord of the Rings author, and even the ANC.

Omaha gets booked out long before the famous AGM, hence my dad's forward planning. The experience gained from being long-term shareholders of Berkshire Hathaway and attending the AGMs, year after year, has influenced my dad's thinking and, therefore, that of the company my parents founded almost twenty years ago. A prime example of this is how Aylett & Co has skin in the game. *Our personal and company wealth is invested alongside that of our investors in the funds we manage, to ensure that our interests are aligned. We eat our own cooking* - Walter Aylett.

The annual Berkshire Hathaway AGM weekend includes the actual meeting, shopping sprees on discounted products from Berkshire businesses, a Nebraska Furniture Mart picnic, and a 5-kilometer Brooks fun run. Attendees can explore the city of Omaha and learn more about Buffett and Munger's backgrounds and lifestyles. Life is simple in Omaha.

On one beautiful, crystal clear morning, I headed to one of Omaha's downtown diners for a traditional breakfast with some Aylett & Co colleagues. There was filter coffee and sassy wisdom served by a typical American waitress, classic tunes flowing from the jukebox in the corner, and fries with breakfast. Yeehaw! We were in cowboy country. I left the diner, walked the Omaha streets, scanned my surroundings, and slowly started comprehending why Omaha worked for Buffett. He says, "Omaha is as good a spot as any. Here you can see the forest. In New York, it's hard to see beyond the trees." (Lowenstein, 1997:125).

Over the years, staff members, clients, and family members have joined the annual trek to Omaha on odd occasions. Clients pay their own way, although my dad makes the arrangements and organizes the coveted AGM meeting passes. Everyone who has made this trip to one of the most attended business events in the world has left with pearls of wisdom shared by the two investment legends.

I interviewed many of these people in 2020 when preparing for this book. What follows are insider accounts from the greatest business event on earth, 'The Warren Buffett and Charlie Munger Show'.

Corné Van Zyl, Investment Analyst at Aylett & Co 2017-2022 (lost his Berkshire virginity in 2018).

Corné grew up in Bloemfontein. In 2011, he read Warren Buffett's biography by Alice Schroeder, The Snowball. He then went on to read The Intelligent Investor by Benjamin Graham. The penny dropped; Corné was hooked. In search of an investment career, it was no surprise that Aylett & Co was the perfect fit. He accompanied my father, a fellow analyst and myself to the 2018 Berkshire Hathaway AGM and had this to say.

When you get to Berkshire, the first thing that hits you is that there's this 85 and 96-year-old on stage and essentially, they are saying the same things they have been saying for the last 50 years. The difference for me now was that I wasn't hearing or seeing these things through a book, a shareholders' letter, or a CNBC interview ... I was watching it live. It struck me that if they have been sticking to the same answers, they must obviously work.

They aren't necessarily geniuses, but they have distilled complex matters to a few essential ideas which they live and operate within. Hearing them at the AGM connected everything I had read about. It was powerful. If someone has been repeating the same idea for 50 years, there must be something to it. I mean, there, Charlie and Warren are getting hammered on a merger debacle on a recent Berkshire purchase, and Warren is word for word using an answer he used 25 years ago in a graduation speech to Harvard graduates. What's more is that even if they repeat a lot, one can still find new golden nuggets of worldly wisdom.

Dimitri Theo, Business Development Manager at Aylett & Co 2017-2023, attended Berkshire in 2019.

You know, when anyone thinks of Buffett, you think of an extremely intelligent person, a typical numbers guy who reads every morning for five hours and considers financial statements as bedtime reading material. He comes across as a nerd who has become one of the best investors of all time. He comes across as a complete numbers person with not much color to him. When I went to go see him in 2019, I realized that there's a hell of a lot more to this person than just numbers and somebody who reads financials.

My biggest takeaway from the Berkshire AGM was that I wished my wife was there with me. Somebody who's not in the financial services industry would have benefited as much as I did. Both Buffett and Munger speak about life. How you live your life is how you invest. I think that's what makes it so simple. They are rational thinkers. When they are confronted with a situation, they respond in a rational manner; whether it concerns their personal lives, or from a work perspective, or an investment point of view.

When you're at the AGM, the penny drops. They are not trying to be complicated. It doesn't feel like I'm at an AGM. I'm not listening to some guy talk about why he's invested in a particular stock for four hours. They're talking to you without having to prepare anything. Everything Warren and Charlie say is because they live what they say. An example of how simple they keep it, was the 2020 AGM being canceled due to COVID-19.

I watched the streamed online AGM; hearing Buffett talk was like listening to a friend because he's so personable. I understand him and get him.

When I got to Aylett & Co, I had an understanding of Buffett and had heard what people said about him, but you don't really appreciate this until you know the core and the essence of the business. In my role as a Business Development Manager, I can't have a vague understanding of Aylett & Co's way of business.

I must have an excellent understanding of what we do and why we do it. I'm the one who sits in front of clients more often than anybody else. I often talk to people at dinner parties about what we do. What you say has got to be genuine. I have to believe that what I'm selling is good. I'm not a second-hand car salesman or an insurance broker who's just going to make you sign on the dotted line and tell you what you want to hear.

Aylett & Co taught me about that honesty. When they invest in a certain way, they tell me why they invest in that way. A lot of it is based on Buffett principles, and they can actually show and explain this to me. That's the big difference.

The business development guy must learn what the investment team is doing and be able to show this to the rest of the world. I can. I know that there's truth and there's honesty and transparency.

When I joined the company, I realized that the team took many principles of Buffett and Munger and didn't merely integrate them into their work lives but also their personal lives. When you first hear of Buffett and what he's accomplished you think he's untouchable, that you can't go see him or talk to him. What's more, you think that the average person who doesn't understand accounting or investing or have simple business knowledge will surely not understand what Buffett talks about and won't benefit from listening to him; and yet when you go there and listen to him, you realize that he is human just like we are.

He does make mistakes, but he tries to think about things as much as he can before he does things; and I think that way of living is what Aylett & Co follows.

We often say to clients, 'Look, we don't know the answer.' We've been very honest. I've never been in a business that's actually said this to clients because most companies will just tell you what they want you to hear. Rather than say, we're not invested in this company because of the following fancy financial ratio reasons, we will say we're not invested in this company because we actually don't understand it.

I think that level of honesty and degree of transparency is something that Buffett and Charlie preach. Last year, when asked about Brexit, both Charlie and Warren stepped in and said, 'Look, to be honest, we don't know what Brexit is. We don't understand it if we don't know all the reasons behind it.

Obviously, we know it's happening, but we're not experts on it; but we will tell you that if we find a good business in the UK that we like, we will go and buy it.'

And so… these guys are human. They don't tell you that they know everything in the world. They know that they know America better than anywhere else. They don't necessarily know everything, but they just focus on the little bit that they do know, their core competence, their circle of competency. And if they can get that right, they're okay. I think that echoes what Aylett & Co does. We are human, we make mistakes. We try to realize what our circle of competence is and if we can do that very well, we'll stick to it.

Zurk Botha, owner of Zurk Botha Associates (Pty) Ltd, a South African Independent Financial Advisory Practice. Seven-time Berkshire Hathaway attendee.

My journey with Buffett started in 2009 when I built up the courage to leave cozy Bloemfontein to set off to the Berkshire Hathaway AGM.

2009 was a difficult year, with the market crash in 2008 and all. We were so motivated to find a truth. We asked ourselves: How has he been doing it all these years?

I went there with the expectation that I would find quick tips and answers; short-term thinking. Immediately when they start talking, you realize there's no short-term, because you're sitting there looking at these guys and they're gray, Ancient, Old men. They sit there and have memories like elephants.

They look at each other and the one says to the other, "Listen, do you remember that stock we bought many years ago at $5.50? Shouldn't have sold that, you know." They're long-term thinkers. You realize it's holistic thinking. You must live it… patience, patience, patience. I think what I've learned from Buffett and Munger is that it takes time and effort to do things. You must have a proper team. You must rely on other people to assist you and you need to take people into your confidence. With a proper team, you let them do what they're good at and you stick to what you're good at and are therefore able to focus on.

I knew someone that went with Walter back in 2005. I didn't have the courage to go then but this person came back saying that he had shaken hands with God. Back then one could still get the chance to meet Warren and get photos.

Your dad has a term, 'We go there to reset our compass to true North.' That phrase refers to more than just sharpening one's investment skills. In 2015 I had the privilege of taking my sons and it was special.

Buffett and Munger teach you about honesty and how they pay their taxes first and then do the rest. I think it's paramount that you study, and you learn, and you keep on learning. I mean if you look at Buffet and Munger, they read every day."

The theme of patience has come up as a prominent one throughout the interviews for this chapter. When I raised this with Zurk and asked what he thought was Buffett's secret, his answer was humorous.

But he has seen it. He's seen it, Kimon. You gotta learn from it... Why would you try to reinvent theory if it's already there. He's done it. He's seen it. So, I think you can't say who's the better guy between Buffett and Charlie. They make a hell of a team, and it's going to be difficult to reproduce that. There will always be somebody next, nobody's irreplaceable. Charlie's brilliant, absolutely brilliant. The way he does things, his comments. The way he handles things; he doesn't waste time. 'I've got nothing to add.' When he does talk, it's short and one often misses it, and you have to go back. In that little line he grumbles, he's given you a whole chapter – in one line. If you've got that kind of skill, shit... you've made it.

When asked what Zurk had most taken away from the AGMs he's attended, other than the virtue of patience, he replied, "*He bought the right company, and that is See's Candies. Peanut brittle will always be the best thing ever...*"

Okay, seriously, it's honesty; you do your part. You conform to the responsibilities you have in the world. I mean that's the thing. If it's the job, you do or your family you look after. In his life Buffett has had his share of family challenges. I think that it's a balancing act you know, you learn from it. He's human after all. Buffett is a personification of capitalism and Berkshire Hathaway's meeting is spectacular.

In business you choose partners. In life what happens is you fall in love with a partner. That's it. And then you deal with whatever comes your way. Now, if there's no more love, then there's no more partnership. I like to be inclusive. I brought my wife to the AGM many times. The insights from the AGM added to our business as well.

- Sex Before 80! -

You know, Buffett shoots from the hip, he says it how it is. Charlie and Buffett are like good cop and bad cop. Warren is kind of smiling, drinking his Coca-Cola and Charlie will just mumble, utter one line and that'll spark a conversation. I always wanted someone from the media to ask me why I came to the AGM? My answer would be, I came for the peanut brittle.

Murray Moore. One of Aylett's investment analysts, stocking up on See's Candies at the 2022 Berkshire Hathaway AGM.

Mel Meltzer, financial adviser for Platinum Portfolios, a South African independent owner-managed fund management company. Three-time Berkshire attendee.

The investment world has always seemed to be quite… what would you call it, you know, quite intimidating in many ways. Going to the shareholders' meeting and sitting in the arena, it dawned on me after listening intently to the two of them, Charlie Munger and Warren Buffett for I think six hours… that investing is actually pure common sense.

My everyday life has changed dramatically because of their teachings. I specifically keep Poor Charlie's Almanack on my desk and often look up stuff in that book and also head back to Snowball. The confidence they give you and the rules they teach you, have made an incredible difference in my life and in my overall outlook. That has saved me a lot of time … a lot of time. Just basic stuff like Warren doesn't buy stuff on auctions. They have saved me so much time in my life, and then just the basic teachings of common sense.

You know, during this difficult time that we are going through (COVID-19 and the poor state of the South African economy), by adhering to their teachings, with one of them being that you don't have to swing at every pitch you receive, is a lesson in itself. Yes, be patient.

You need to understand what you're investing in. It gives one a lot of confidence to be patient, regardless of the circumstances, if things don't make sense to you. In many ways in my life, it has given me an anchor of sorts.

Buffett has been conservative. He's not going to be rushing out and buying stuff because the Treasury's buying up all these assets.

Yes sir, it gives one a lot of comfort by sticking to the principles. If you look at our returns that we've generated at Platinum Portfolios, we have not generated those returns by being clever.

We have not generated those returns by being in and out of stocks daily. We've generated those returns by simply trying to implement the rules and caveats that have been laid down by Munger and Buffett.

For example, I was thinking earlier today: Buffett is absolutely amazing. Here's a guy who's 89 years old, who in this environment is still trying to perfect the tapestry of investing that he started in 1948, because he is so patient. What guy at 89 can be as patient as that? His principles are much more important than the short-term stuff and he sticks to those principles properly.

As told by Robert Miles, author of the Warren Buffett CEO, in his interview with Alec Hogg. *People can relate to Warren with his Midwestern attitudes and values, his character, his reputation and the fact that he speaks the truth. No other CEO has quite the draw that Warren Buffett has. One can get a chance to meet him, for example, he's not untouchable. He has lots of jokes – he could easily be a 77-year-old stand- up comedian.*

He had me on the floor with extraordinary insights and very funny answers to questions like, 'if you could have one publication delivered on a deserted island, which publication would it be?' He interrupted me and said, "A publication? I thought I'd get a person on a deserted island." (Miles, YouTube 2008)

Alec Hogg, Financial journalist, founder of BizNews.com, and author of How To Invest Like Warren Buffett: Discover the Wisdom of the World's Greatest Wealth Creator. Nine-time Berkshire Hathaway attendee.

I only really got to know about Warren in 2006. What happened was that Kokkie Koyman, one of South Africa's top investment specialists, and Laurie Dippenaar, self-made South African businessman, investor and banker, invited me to come along to the Berkshire Hathaway AGM. They stressed that one didn't know how much longer Warren and Charlie would carry on for. Warren Buffett's not getting any younger and Charlie Munger, in particular, was already 80 years old. The AGM is a 'bit of Americana', was the way that they described it. They said you can only come if, first, you have read Roger Lowenstein's book Making of an American Capitalist, which is a wonderful primer on Buffett.

After reading that, I couldn't wait to get to Omaha. So, I went for the first time in 2006. It was probably the greatest gift that those two gents gave me ... to introduce me to these extraordinary human beings. I guess it's been a journey since then.

What happened to me was that after discovering Mr. Buffett and Mr. Munger, Warren and Charlie as the world knows them, it completely changed my mind about so many things. I wrote a lot of the advice down, having gone to each of the Berkshire AGMs from 2006 to 2012. I had reams of notes that were taken at the AGMs and in the press conferences I was lucky enough to get into. What kept me going back, was that there's almost a mini industry that has now evolved around the AGM.

Suddenly, in 2012, I was no longer part of MoneyWeb – the business that was supposed to be my life's work. I'd spent 15 years there and it was quite a shock for it to have ended.

I had to decide what to do. There were a lot of very smart people who guided me, but the best guidance I had was from Buffett and Munger. They didn't even know about this because I had pulled out my notebooks and started reading through the wisdom, they had shared over all those years. It eventually ended up in a book that I wrote in 2016 - How to Invest like Warren Buffett.

It got my mind completely focused on what I wanted to do with my life. Part of what they say is to try and do something that you're the best in the world at. On the one hand, invest in yourself. Secondly, try and invest in a way that you can become the best in the world ... at one thing, at something. You have the chance to be the best in the world in a very small, little area, which is your circle of competence. They talk a lot about this 'circle of competence'.

It got me to realize that up to that point, I had spent a career in financial journalism. What could I be the best in the world at and how great it would be if I could expand that and start a business with the global South African in mind, or the 'global mind' of South Africa. Our country had been very insular over many years. I saw an opportunity in bringing in information from other parts of the world.

I just saw how much interest my trips to Omaha had engendered among people who read MoneyWeb, so I thought, why don't you just do this on a global basis. So, if it wasn't for Warren and Charlie, BizNews would never have happened. That's yet another example of how their teachings influenced me. It wasn't as if they sat down and said anything to me directly, but it's about what they share with the world. If you're able to apply that to your own life it can make a massive difference.

Researching and writing my book, was a way of getting more people to understand that these incredible, incredible human beings, are role models in life. Generally, the humility, the understanding and appreciation of how the world locks together, and how little we know, is the beginning of wisdom. Like Socrates once said, 'I know nothing'.

The first time I went, obviously I knew nothing. I then saw that there were press badges around; so, I then applied for and got press accreditation. That entitled me to go with about 30 accredited people to a special press conference which was held on the Sunday morning, where each of us got to ask Warren and Charlie a question. People queued the whole night to try and get close to the microphones, so they could maybe get the opportunity in the five-hour AGM to pose a question to Warren and Charlie.

So, if you have special press access as an incentive, well... that means that you booked your ticket immediately because to have it is a privilege. It's *just massive! At that press conference, you effectively got a few hours of 30 questions being asked of these two, who weren't anywhere else right then, so you absolutely needed to be there.*

There is a whole subculture where one has the ability to engage with other, really, really smart value investors. There were conferences held around the time that I used to attend, which added enormous value to my education. It was almost a bootcamp in capitalism; showing how capitalism should and does work. Attending the press conference was my annual highlight.

I would always go and sit right in the front row, as close as possible, get my microphone and the recording going. Then, after the 30 questions had been asked, what would happen is we'd all kind of mob them on the table. They'd sit there and you'd go around them, and they'd sign dollar bills and reports and caps, and you'd be able to throw questions in a less formal environment.

One year, I managed to have my photograph taken with Charlie and Warren. I keep that photo in my private office. Daily, that photo reminds me of my North Star, and it advises me in this or that circumstance.

The one thing that shines through is their humility, their absolute, incredible humility. They explain it simply on the basis that if you need a Greek letter in a formula to decide about investments, then you're making a mistake. It's really so much of life in their minds, that often the answers are quite simple and obvious. As Buffett says, 'you don't have to know if a person is 310 pounds or 320 pounds to know they're fat.'

So, Buffett and Munger reckon that business schools should dispense with the whole curriculum and only teach models of real events that have happened, taking a test case of an Enron for real life experience of companies… That's what you should be learning, rather than some guy's view of what the world is, because they say that the big trends are impossible to predict. The big picture is very difficult and impossible to forecast.

The place where you can understand with a high degree of certainty is... when you have a look at a business, and you understand the business model. When Buffett bought Apple, it was the very first share that he'd ever bought which had a technology bias to it, but he had Bill Gates on his board of directors, from Microsoft... So why didn't he buy Microsoft shares?

He said he didn't know enough about it. That's the humility of the man, he probably knows more about Microsoft than you and I could ever dream of today. When he knows a share, he can predict with a relative degree of certainty what its earnings are going to be in the next five years. One thinks of how few investors can predict, with a degree of certainty, what a company's earnings are going to be in the next year. Investing to him isn't going to be a string of Greek letters. It's going to be based on some common sense and on the understanding that the biggest obstacle to investing is emotion.

Buffett often refers to Benjamin Graham's book, The Intelligent Investor. He says that there are really two major parts to that book, two magic chapters. One is the chapter on Mr. Market, which gets you to understand why there's so much volatility in the share market and that the share market is there to serve you, not the other way around. The other chapter is about a margin of safety: so when you do work out the intrinsic value of what you believe is a company's worth and you're happy to become a co-owner in the company at that price, you need a margin of safety - probably 2 percent.

Once you understand those two concepts, you can invest. You don't let your emotions take you off track. Now that's maybe an hour's lecture max at the universities. Well yeah, what is the lecturer going to do for the rest of the academic year?

Taking a look at Warren Buffett's performance. For 50 years he's done this! and he's got a 20 percent compound annual growth rate which means that his investments have grown by 20 percent, taking account of the beginning value and the end value, assuming that the profits were reinvested at the end of every year of the investment's lifespan. He never talks about his investment achievements, and he doesn't respond when people attack him.

When you read his annual letters to shareholders, he consistently starts off by trumpeting his failures and being very quiet about his successes. That's a result of humility, which creates the road to open-mindedness and to learning. Buffett keeps learning. He keeps talking about this circle of competence and expanding his circle of competence, learning more and reading more.

Susie Buffett would say Warren's idea of heaven is going upstairs with a hamburger and a Coke and a pack of annual reports to read through.

The great thing is that you don't have to sit with Buffett to learn from him. You can learn from him by reading or by just seeing the way he operates… but primarily it's his humility… it's that ability not to take himself very seriously. It's the ability to point out his mistakes and he does this in every report you read. Rather than trumpeting our successes, if we can trumpet our failures, this keeps us humble, it keeps us growing, it keeps us learning. I would say that that's probably going to be the most important chapter in your book.

Laurie Dippenaar, Ex-Chairman and Co-Founder of FirstRand, Africa's largest listed financial services group (by market capitalization). Six-time Berkshire Hathaway attendee.

I had heard about Buffett or had read about him. Still, my first Berkshire meeting was due to Kokkie Kooyman inviting me. The one condition for me going was to have read The Making of an American Capitalist by Roger Lowenstein. This was very sound advice as I didn't arrive at Berkshire stone cold.

That book was my first proper introduction. I enjoyed that meeting so much that it led me to attend several further Berkshire meetings. At Berkshire, you're witnessing a little bit of American history.

It's unheard of, 40,000 odd people attending an AGM. I mean FirstRand is a reasonably big company. When you take out our staff numbers at an AGM, roughly four outsiders are remaining. I personally do not think the numbers will continue once Warren and Charlie have passed. They'll make a movie about it one day. It is a bit like a cult movement... One would religiously be directed to Gorat's, Warren's favorite steakhouse.

Obviously, what struck me at the meeting was the incredible clarity of their thinking. It is so simple and so rational, an uncomplicated type of thinking. And this thing that it's either a simple "yes" or "no" or "too difficult" decision. They stick to what they believe in, and they don't get distracted by a rabbit running across the path. I also feel that I can relate to their long-term thinking. I like to own shares that I don't have to sell. What also stands out for me is their humility. Buffett drives the same old car. I mean, when he needed a new car, he asked his wife to buy one, and she said, 'Well, what car?' and he said, 'Well, I don't have time to choose a car, just get a green one.' It didn't matter to him, as long as the car had four wheels and could go.

At one meeting, he was asked a question and he simply said that he didn't know the answer. There is nothing worse than someone who shoots their mouth off and acts like they know something about everything. Even though Warren Buffett is who he is, he can distinguish what he knows and doesn't know.

He has this ability to be frank in a manner that is not insulting or defensive. What truly impacted me, is his way of simplifying matters, to truly crystallize the real issues. Essentially keeping things simple and not trying to complicate matters.

I feel that I've been somewhat successful at that. The other thing is the question of long-term matters and long-term thinking. He's an incredibly logical person. I mean when it comes to describing their remuneration practice, you know in the company, he simply bases it on something logical, and you think to yourself that's an absurd way to reward yourself. When making investment decisions, he's able to take out emotion completely. I've really tried to emulate Buffett, in applying incredible logic to my decision-making.

Warren and Charlie's integrity resonated with me. This complete trust, I mean… I own a reasonable amount of Berkshire Hathaway shares and I never worry for a nanosecond that I'll be prejudiced as a minority shareholder; and a big thing these days is the independence of directors. If you've been a director for nine years, okay, you're no longer independent because you own too many shares in the company, and therefore, you're not classified as independent.

Remember, independence comes from independence of thought. For Bill Gates, who's on the board of Berkshire Hathaway, and earns a considerable board position fee per year the fee is immaterial to him. Now that's someone else who ticks all the independence boxes. Often the risk is that directors won't stand up to management because they don't want to get taken off the board and lose the salary that goes with the position.

I think that Warren and Charlie have an incredibly disciplined approach to investments. One may have a portfolio that is opportunistic with a shorter time horizon, but that hasn't done well. What's really done well are the ones that I've been in long- term and have held onto over the years.

Yes, they've had some bad investments, which were sound at the time and just didn't work out.

It wasn't because they were speculative. Whereas most investors have short time horizons, I made my money in investing in banking for 40 odd years... It took a very long time. You should always start off with integrity and trust, be incredibly logical about your investment decision and be committed long-term. Charlie is hilarious. I think he's also a great example of humility. The number of times he's said, 'I've got nothing to add ...' He gives the impression of an equally highly intelligent man who is in sync with Warren, and someone who is not fazed about being number two. That is the maturity of Mr. Munger."

Piet Viljoen, Executive Director and Portfolio Manager of Counterpoint Asset Manager, a South African-based multi-strategy asset management business. Six-time Berkshire Hathaway AGM attendee.

I read a book on Buffett and then I started reading his annual reports and shareholder letters. Then I said, well, hang on, they've got this annual shareholders' meeting. At that stage probably about 2,000 or 3,000 people were going to it and I thought maybe it'd be a good idea to go across to Omaha and check it out myself. I think it was 1996 when I went. Over a period of 10 years, I went five times. Of course, I didn't know what to expect at all. I flew to Omaha, and I stayed in some funny hotel that I forget the name of. It was sort of off a back street. At that stage the meeting itself was held in a stadium that was used for rodeos and for cattle shows and that sort of thing. You know it would take probably about 2,000 people or so. There were some overflow tents outside where you could sit and watch on big screen TVs. Stalls for all the different companies were, you know, outside there.

You could walk around and listen to what was going on. So, there's just the idea to immerse myself in the whole set up and the whole experience without any explanation at all. Which I thought was quite useful. Yeah, I think the main thing was that these guys cut out all the bullshit and kept it very simple and clear and consistent. There was nothing fancy and there was no fancy math's or fancy science. It was just basic, fundamental common sense, applied in a very practical way, as opposed to all the management speak you always read and hear regurgitated by professional management teams of listed companies.

If I was a university lecturer, I would run a course on Buffett and Munger. The textbook I would use would be The Essays of Warren Buffett: Lessons for Investors and Managers by Lawrence Cunningham, where he takes all the shareholders' letters and sort of amalgamates them by topic. The Berkshire AGM would pull you back again and again. You know, every time you went there, you would pick up something else. Also, at the time, more and more South Africans started going, so it was a nice networking opportunity as well. You got a combination of learning from Warren and Charlie. After a while, there was nothing new from that side. Then it became more of a networking opportunity with other like-minded investors, which I found quite useful.

Saying it is one thing and doing it is another. That's where my fascination with Warren and Charlie started. They have done it over a period of 60 years: they have consistently done what they said they would do, and I think that's almost unique in the world. I don't think there's any other institution that I know of that is able to do that over such a long period of time. You put them up there and you try and emulate what they've done.

At our company we write a letter to our shareholders which tries to be as open as possible and to disclose as much as shareholders are entitled to know. So, there's a practical example of what we do in terms of trying to emulate them.

. . . .

Walter Aylett, Founder of Aylett & Co Fund Managers, twenty-one times Berkshire attendee.

My first meeting was in '99 and I have missed one. 2022 was my 20th Berkshire Hathaway AGM.

I mean, Corné is a great example. Here is a young man from Bloemfontein, the South African version of Omaha, whose life has been influenced by two elderly investors halfway across the world. Corné invested on behalf of family and friends at a young age and what's more, he would write annual letters to his 'shareholders' emulating Berkshire's style. I'm not trying to live the way Buffett and Munger live their lives. I respect their principles and that these principles don't change. Their principles can be used by everyone; and it's not only Buffett and Munger I got to see. There were other people there whom I met, other fund managers, where I would think ... we all belong to the same church, if you want to call it that. We speak the same language. Paul Lountzis, a fantastic Greek, was one such person I met at an AGM. Both being Greek, we shared something in common and I'll probably see him there once a year. He's a wonderful man and we're very similar in the way we think. He's incredibly focused.

It's quite nerve-racking to go to Omaha from South Africa. It's an incredibly far way to travel. You must organize accommodation far in advance. Typically, you've invited one or two clients or friends to go with you. Although they pay for themselves, you're responsible for getting them there. That can be quite a logistical nightmare. You're doing 30-hour trips in the air to get there for literally two days before getting back on a plane to return home, unless you add on some time in America to go see my family and visit companies. You know, it's hard to go from Cape Town to Dubai, Dubai to Chicago or London to Chicago, and then to catch another plane to Omaha. You literally leave South Africa on a Tuesday and get there on a Wednesday American time – after 30 hours of flying. It's not only having to sit still for all that time, but you're also jet lagged *and still trying to run your business, have a career and make sure everyone is happy. Then you've got clients who fly in at different times.*

You ask yourself: 'why go to all this trouble to organize this trip?' You always say this is in the beginning: 'I'm not going to do this again, it's too difficult.' However, by the end of the trip you're saying to yourself, 'Ah I can't wait for the next one!' It's just got better and better.

As a result, there's not even a discussion now of the logistical nightmare you go through. It's also become quite expensive because the hotels have taken advantage of the AGM. Airlines have taken advantage of it. So, it's an expensive exercise for a South African to go with the weak currency that we have. But I can say it's like a refresher course, your behavior gets positively reinforced all the time.

The next part that's really exciting leading up to the AGM, which has got bigger and bigger every year; is meeting people and sharing ideas. There's a university that runs a business school with one and two-day courses where you meet other fund managers, so there's almost a jamboree feel, a festival feeling. You've got the shopping that you get to do, which is great. You get a 20 percent discount as a shareholder. And then you get into the AGM meeting and that in itself is the second hurdle, you wake up at 5:30, rush to the venue and then queue outside for two hours to get your seat. Sometimes it rains and again you ask yourself what the hell you're doing there. But then you sit down and seven hours later, you all look at each other and say, "Wow". You're not necessarily learning new things. Buffett and Munger's answers are so damn consistent. You know the answer they're going to give before they even open their mouths because they are so consistent. They got to that answer when they were 8 years old. They never lie, so there are no lies for them to remember. You get all these principles from Buffett and Munger and I think that's what I get out of it. And of course, after the meeting, you all go to a steakhouse, especially since Omaha is known for its meat.

Everyone is jovial, and we all enjoy the camaraderie and the atmosphere. There is a collective wisdom and an 'abundance' mentality; competitors are with you, clients and suppliers, all South African. Sometimes we've had tables of twenty people in a restaurant. When you get back on the plane to leave you get reminded about the sheer size of America and the sheer power of the American economy, which Buffett talks about at length. So, it's simply a wonderful experience, just to remind yourself of these principles of the Midwest way of thinking; the way Buffett and Munger talk, keeping it simple. The reason why they are so good is that they can make themselves understood – because they really know what they are talking about. You cannot simplify something into two lines if you don't understand it. That's what Buffett is good at; he has this wonderful ability to simplify complex things."

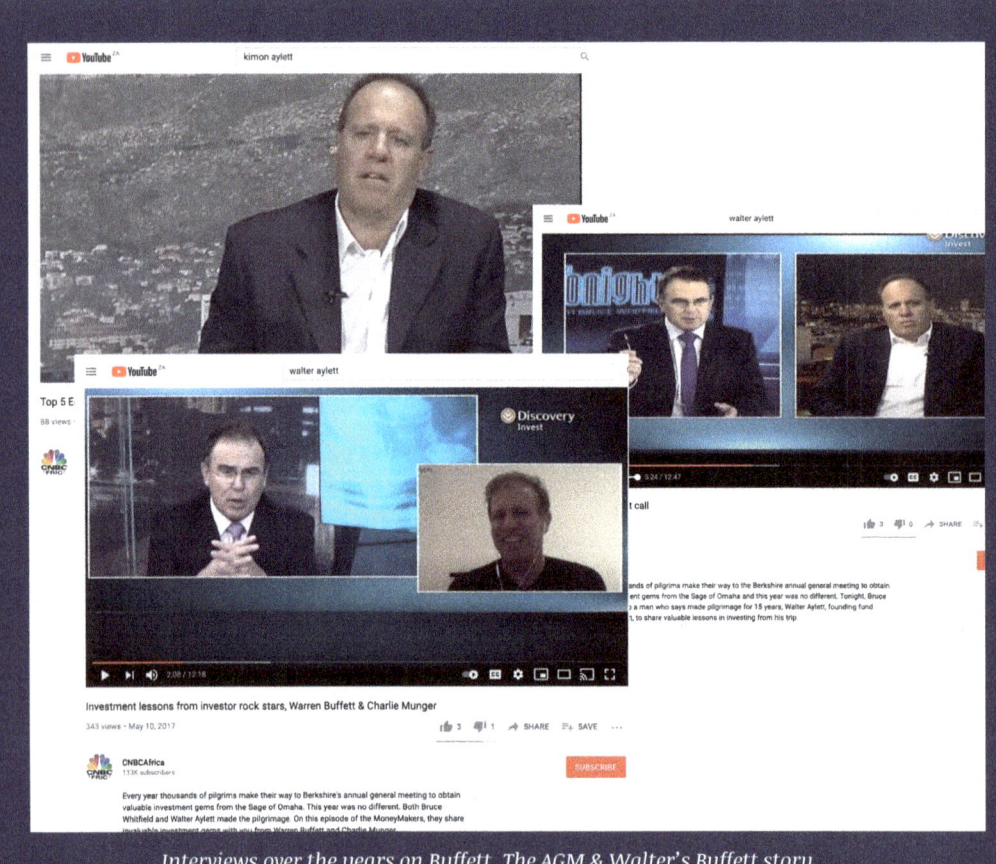

*Interviews over the years on Buffett, The AGM & Walter's Buffett story.
Source: YouTube.*

I think Charlie's affected me much more in my personal life. Buffett has influenced me more in my investment philosophy, and it's not only Buffett. It's people like Benjamin Graham, friends of Buffett and of course, Charlie. Bear in mind that being in South Africa, we have different market conditions to those in the States. We must adapt. We learn from Buffett and his cronies. Charlie has definitely helped me in my personal life, with things like humility and modesty. In some respects, Charlie is not a humble or a modest guy… but you know the way he always refers to Buffett as being smarter shows he's not arrogant. He doesn't want to take the praise; he pushes it toward Buffett.

The money doesn't go to their heads. They still flew economy class until it was too difficult due to being swamped by fellow passengers. They still go to cheap restaurants. Certainly Buffett does. I also think that it's fine to be different. Charlie says you should spend the money, enjoy it, whereas Buffett doesn't, he's quite tight. Midwest rules, you know, that was the thing. Both Buffett and Munger come from Omaha. A large proportion of their upbringing was in that Midwest way of thinking. When I first took you to Omaha for your 16th birthday, I was trying to introduce you to these principles. I just think of the wisdom I have gained from the principles of investing and the principles of being a good human being that I have learned from Buffett and Munger.

If my son wanted to start a business, I'd say look at Mrs. B, who ran Nebraska Furniture Mart and ask: Why did she succeed? She was a Russian immigrant who didn't have any university education, but she knew the customer, she knew her product. She worked very, very hard, 20 hours a day. Anyone can be successful in business; you don't necessarily need to be super-educated. Unfortunately, South African universities and most tertiary education institutions don't encourage us to think like this. It just seems too simple and perhaps academics don't like it because they can't write long textbooks on Buffett type ideas. It's too commonsense, it's too rational. After three months you've done Buffett and you don't have to do anything else. Universities want you there for four years.

They want to teach you about stuff that doesn't even exist, like The Efficient Market Theory. It holds that investment markets reflect all known public information and that it's impossible for an investor to beat the market. In my opinion that is useless information.

I think practical, relevant content is such an important part of learning. Of course, there'll be other equally important Buffett's and Munger's to read about and learn about. I think what Buffett does really well is saying the way he sees it in a very simple way. Munger refers to so many telling examples of success and failure in his book. If you really want to do well in business, be rational, have a commonsense approach to decision-making in business, delight your customer and you will be successful. Work hard and have integrity. I think Charlie is beyond ethics. He once bought a small minority share from the last shareholder in the bank before he delisted the company. It was from an old woman. He overpaid for the stock because he didn't want to be seen as doing her in. When you can live your life like that, you get things that you deserve. In other words, if you do things of a deserving nature, good things happen to you. So, it's wise to be more conservative in your taxes. Don't take shortcuts, call it out if it's close to the line. Be tough on yourself, have high standards. Read every day. Hire smart, good people. By far the biggest lesson at Aylett & Co is that I made one very, very good decision. I hired the nicest, hardest working, ethical, well-mannered people. I say that because I see how they treat their families and their spouses and one another. They're willing to share their bonuses and don't accept bad behavior. When you want to start a family, a club, a business… if you can apply those principles and earn trust, you will go far in life.

*The divorce was a massive thing for my family. I hope that my kids will look back one day and say that their father, despite those difficult circumstances and the pressure that he faced, never let them down. That he was there for them, that he was fair to his ex-wife and that he had integrity. I am probably considered to be a very difficult man, but I do my best to be very good to people and to my staff. Have a stoic philosophy. Take it on the chin – no one is going to feel sorry for you. That's life, it happens, doesn't matter how bad it is, do not feel sorry for yourself. If you display behavior of a deserving nature, it will get back to you. If you sleep with dogs, you will get fleas. Stick with good people and good things will happen. Be fair, be tough, but at the same time you're a human being. I don't know the human side of Buffett and Munger but what I have seen and read…
I would like to be like them in their public lives. I'm not sure about their personal lives. I do like how Munger takes his family to his big house for*

reunions. Warren and Charlie are adapting all the time, they're learning machines. Something that was an anathema five years ago, they're doing today. They are not changing their principles; they're just educating themselves. Warren can't help himself. He loves the game; it's not about making money. He wants to compete, and he's fascinated by how a business operates.

Every year, your papou used to ask me about the Berkshire Hathaway share price. He wasn't exactly the investor type who kept up with the stock market.

I started to wonder why he kept asking me about it. One day, I asked him why, and he told me that he had secretly purchased six Berkshire shares. He planned to leave one share in his will to each of his grandchildren.

When I asked him what made him buy those shares, he simply replied, "Well, you visited this bunch yearly…it must be a good investment."

Kimon & Walter at the Berkshire Hathaway AGM 2018 & 2022.

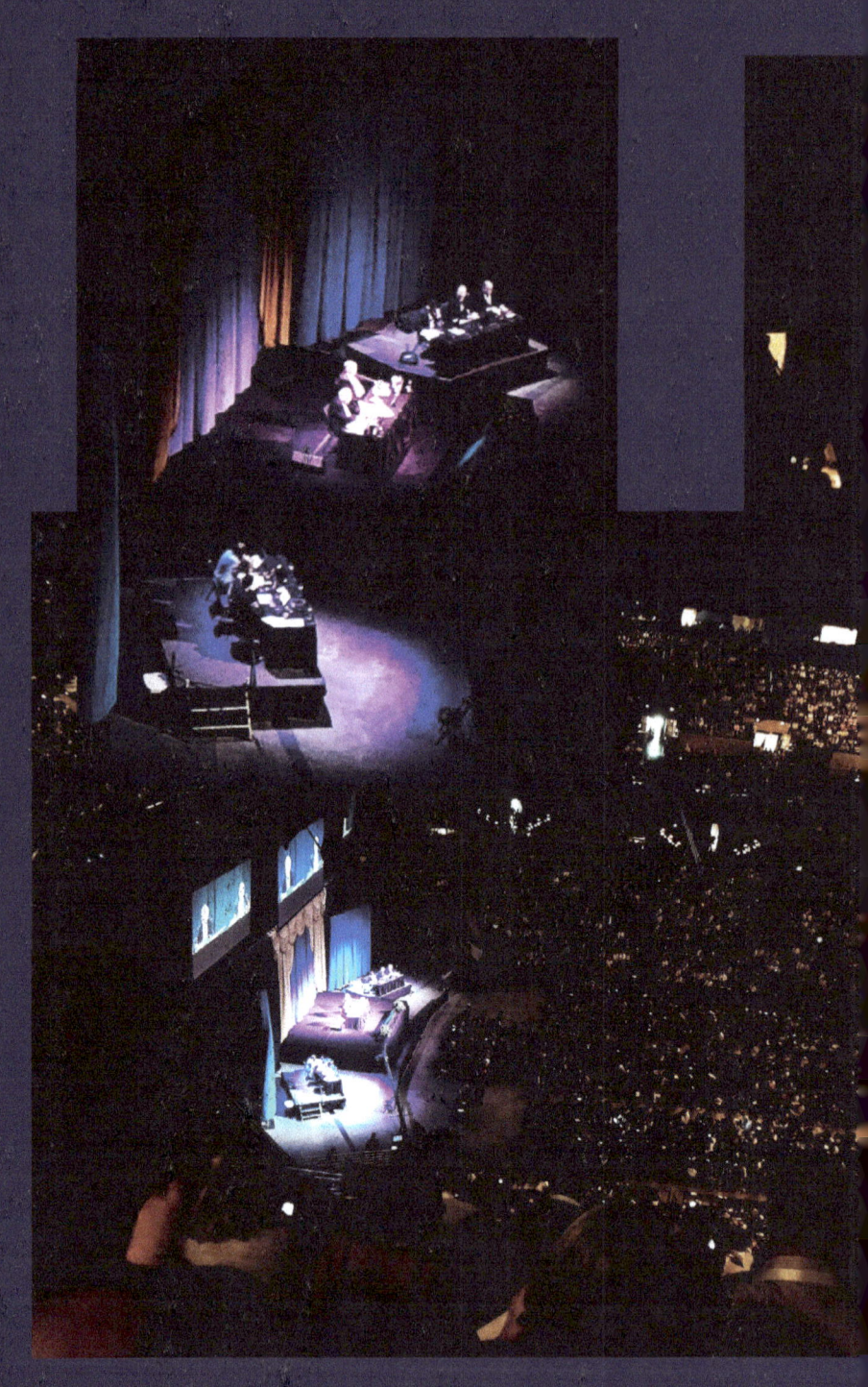

Berkshire Hathaway AGM 2018.

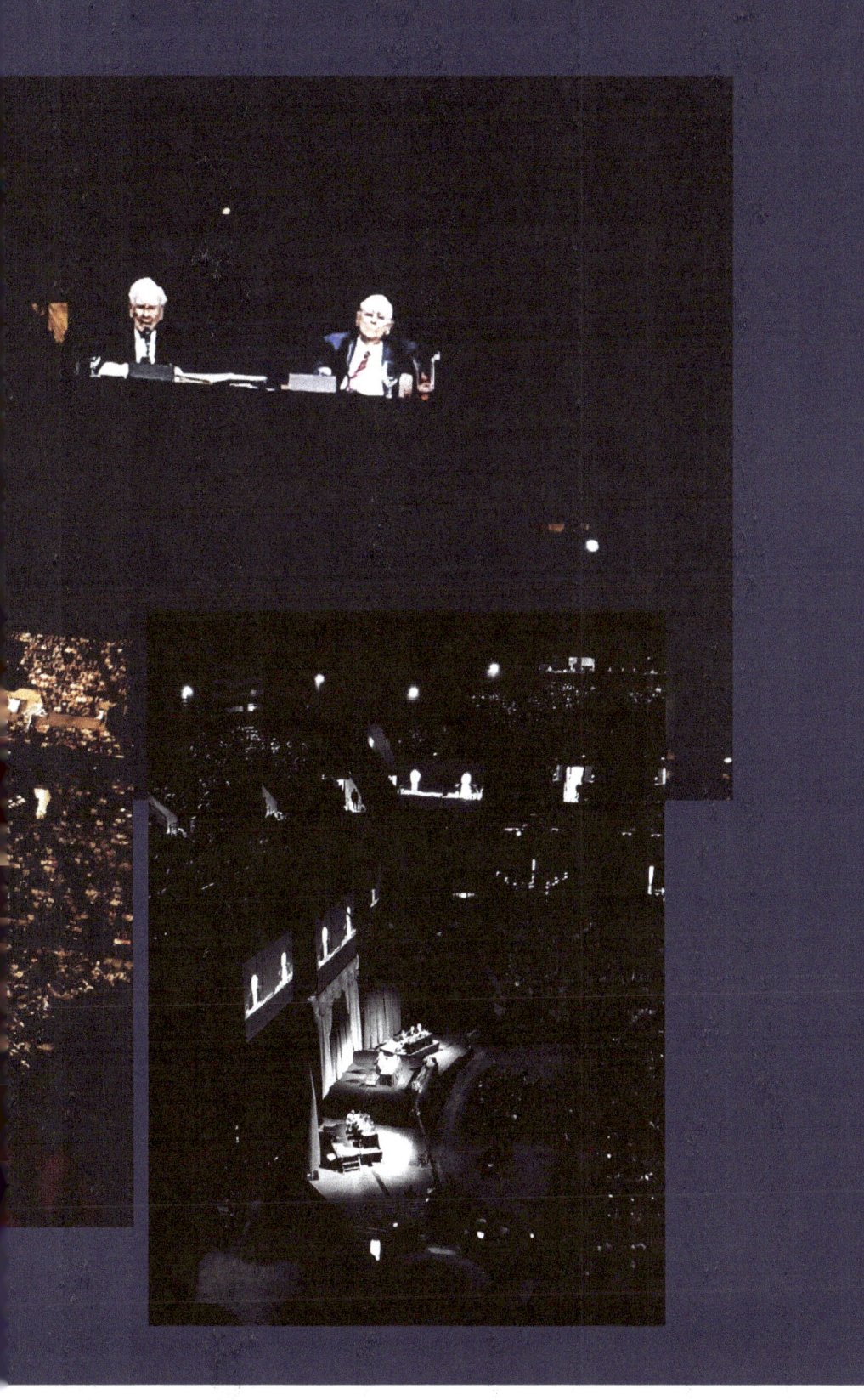

Walter and Kimon at the recent Berkshire Hathaway AGM 2022. Warren and Charlie back at their familiar in-person positions with Greg Abel and Ajit Jain.

Kimon, Walter and Murray Moore braving the cold at six a.m. in the famous Berkshire Queue, 2022.

Six a.m. Berkshire Queue, 2022.

Walter & Justin Ritchie completing the Brooks Invest in Yourself 5K 2015.

Walter & Dimitri Theo enjoying a steak at Buffett's usual lunch spot, Gorat's, 2019.

Walter and Kimon outside the Brooks stand at Berkshire Hathaway AGM 2018.

Walter and Dimitri Theo with Poor Charlie's Almanack, 2019.

Zurk Botha, Walter and Dimitri Theo at Berkshire Hathaway AGM 2019.

CHAPTER 7 – LIKE-MINDED, FOCUSED INDIVIDUALS

"You will move in the direction of the people that you associate with. So, it's important to associate with people that are better than yourself... you want to associate with people who are the kind of person you'd like to be."
– Warren Buffett.

In any school, university, or work environment, it doesn't take long for the talented to attract one another. Talented can mean good-looking, popular, or being smart. Subconsciously you start mixing with like-minded individuals. Jock with jock. Nerd with nerd. Popular kids versus geeky kids. I am fascinated by how certain individuals, each talented in their own special way, became friends. When they are seen sharing dinner and spending time together, one is not surprised at their friendship.

Good examples of such friendships among celebrities are actors Brad Pitt and Leonardo Di Caprio, often seen with matching Starbucks Frappuccinos going for a walk in Central Park. Tennis giants Roger Federer and Rafael Nadal played countless exhibitions together, giggled like school kids throughout the points, and even texted each other congrats after a big grand slam win.

Then, of course, there is the friendship between Bill Gates, business magnate, software developer and philanthropist and Warren Buffett, business mogul, philanthropist and one of the most successful investors in the world. Warren was 60 and Bill 35 when they met in July 1991 at a dinner.

At the 2000 Berkshire Hathaway AGM, Buffett shared the story of how they met. He was visiting the state of Washington to see a very good friend, Meg Greenfield, editorial page editor at the Washington Post. She had contacted him a year or two previously to ask his advice about whether she could afford to buy a second home. At the time, he stopped her from sending him her financial information saying, "Meg, you don't need to. Anybody that asks me whether they can afford something can afford it.

It's the people that don't ask me that can never afford it. Just go do it. It'll make you happy". Meg bought her home and invited Buffett to come out for the July 4th weekend in 1991 and see what she'd done.

It so happened that she was a friend of Bill's parents who invited Warren to dinner during his visit to Washington State. The tech billionaire's mother felt strongly that the two should meet to the point of insisting on it. Bill was reluctant and tried to get out of the dinner, telling his mother, *"Mom, I'm busy!"*

I didn't even want to meet Warren because I thought, 'Hey, this guy buys and sells things, and so he found imperfections in terms of markets, that's not value added to society, that's a zero-sum game that is almost parasitic.' That was my view before I met him … he wasn't going to tell me about inventing something (cnbc.com).

According to Buffett, Gates wasn't interested in meeting him but rather Kay Graham, who was also attending the dinner. Katherine (Kay) Graham headed up her family's newspaper, The Washington Post, from 1963 to 1991 and supported the paper's investigation into the Watergate scandal. The political scandal, the biggest in the history of the US, led to the resignation of President Richard Nixon (Britannica, 2022).

Gates simply felt that he and Buffett operated too differently in the world of business for there to be any value in their meeting and sharing insights — Buffett is an investor looking to create value for himself and his shareholders, while Gates, especially at that point in Microsoft's history, was more focused on building software that would change the way people and businesses use computers in their daily lives.

He finally agreed to spend no more than a couple of hours at the dinner, but once the two men met, Gates was hooked. Their dinner conversation convinced him Buffett had plenty to offer, and they talked for several hours.

I realize everything he does is based on a framework of the world where he's judging — judging markets, judging people, judging how things work, in a very deep way... I realized [that] although we come from different places, we're both trying to model the world and what goes on (cnbc.com). - Bill Gates.

That dinner sparked what has now been a three-decade friendship between the two billionaires. *The dinner began an unbelievable friendship for me, and I could tell that even though we came from different directions, the kinds of things that fascinated us and that we thought were important were very much the same,* Gates told business students at the University of Nebraska in 2006 (cnbc.com).

In addition to their friendship, Gates and Buffett joined forces in 2010 to announce the Giving Pledge campaign, whereby the pair recruited over 200 wealthy people worldwide to donate the bulk of their fortunes to philanthropic causes. Buffett has also donated considerable amounts to the Bill and Melinda Gates Foundation, more than $36 billion since 2006.

Warren always says his primary aim was to commit his resources to improve the health and welfare of others who have not had the same opportunities and luck he has. His gift has done that and more. It has helped to save literally millions of lives – from the provision of life-saving vaccines to treatments and protection from deadly diseases like HIV, TB, and malaria. His generosity has helped millions of people lift themselves and their families out of extreme poverty globally, through its work in agricultural development and financial inclusion, it has deepened and accelerated work in the United States to advance educational opportunities for people of color, minority groups and low-income students.

Through the Giving Pledge, Warren has also worked with Bill and Melinda to encourage more than 200 billionaires to commit to giving away at least half their wealth. The ripple effects are incalculable.

- Mark Suzman - CEO, Board Member, Bill & Melinda Gates Foundation (Gates Foundation, 2022).

What is also incredible about Buffett is the amount of his fortune that he's giving away. I don't think many people appreciate and honestly understand how much of his fortune is given away to charity. He doesn't put it under the Warren Buffett name but gives it to the Bill and Melinda Gates Foundation because he'll say, 'why change something that works well?' and he doesn't want his name in lights. Two of the richest men in the world are giving away most of their fortunes. He's not looking to reinvent the wheel and he's giving away all that money without expecting any sort of recognition for it. I think that's incredible. Gates and Buffett are both very smart, love knowledge, read voraciously and enjoy playing bridge (online with each other). One of the first things Buffett noticed about Bill Gates is that he was incredibly focused, something that's essential if one is to succeed in business. One must be able to recognize when something important or significant is happening. It is easier to focus if you love what you're doing, because then you will have the mental strength to shut out unnecessary stimuli. - Laurie Dippenaar.

* * * * * * * * * * * * *

The reason why I think asset management can fail badly at times, is that in this industry there are very clever people and sometimes they're too damn clever. They think their competence never ends and that they're competent in everything and that's simply not true. We are all only good at certain things and we need to be focused.

When Gates and Buffett met for the first time, Buffett saw Gates from the other side of the table and the way he was talking immediately resonated with Buffett. Gates was incredibly focused. Being too focused on one thing has its drawbacks, however. You must maintain a balance so that you do not shut out important aspects of your social life, such as family.

Roger Federer is an excellent example of an international celebrity whose energy, drive and ambition enables him to remain focused, while at the same time not neglecting his family. His wife, Mirka, and his parents, Lynette and Robert Federer, form his main support system.

Warren Buffett has his first wife, Susie Buffett, to thank for initially being his support. When she left him, she asked her friend, Astrid, to go and live with him and organize his life. Buffett needed that support because he worked hard and focused deeply, immersing himself in his business.

For the rest of the evening when Warren and Bill met, they carried on talking to each other as if no one else existed. You can only do that if you're focused. It's tantamount to me talking to you right now. I can just see you. I can't see the wall, I can't see the dog, it's focused vision; and clearly, if you have that ability to shut out everything else and be focused, you'll stand a good chance of succeeding in business and in life.

It requires mental strength, it's a discipline. It is a process that you go through. So, what is that one thing that makes someone be selected as one of eleven players for the South African cricket team, from an entire country of 50 million people? You find that it's those people who are incredibly focused and have this ability to shut out all the noise. Yes, they know how to play the stroke and they know what to do, but it's their incredible focus to recognize when something important or significant is happening, and in that moment, to know what to do.

Buffett was very focused. He worked out a philosophy, starting with the teachings of value investing by Benjamin Graham. Later, Munger came along with quality investing. Using his own analogy, Buffett knew the exact quadrants in the pitching/hitting zone. He is so focused on "the ball" in those quadrants, that he smacks it as hard as he can, because he knows he's going to hit a home run. And that's what I learned about being focused. It's about getting rid of all the chaff, all the noise, and being singularly focused on the task at hand. It is a very hard thing to do.

Federer, the tennis player, is very focused. It's his energy, ambition… he loves what he does. If you love what you do, it's easier to be focused; and to be very good at something you must be focused. When you try to do too many things, you lose that focus. You can't deal with all the *stimuli being thrown at you. I actually think the best way to get focused is the ability to say No a lot. If you say no to a lot of things, you end up looking at what you enjoy the most and hence what you're focusing on.*

The other side of the coin is that you get so focused that you block out too many things, such as family. For example, when Buffett came home from the business day, he would go straight upstairs to his study and read. If he had his lamp, an annual report and a burger, he was happy. But meanwhile, downstairs was his family dying to spend time with him. The question is: how do you successfully balance this work focus and the rest of your life?

Often, unfortunately, the process of success demands excessive focus, to the detriment of other aspects of life. One of the reasons that Susie Buffett asked her friend Astrid, to live with Warren when she left him, was that he was so focused in his tunnel vision that he wouldn't have known where to switch the lights on in the house. He literally didn't know. Sometimes people accuse me of being disinterested or think I'm not listening and it's because I'm deeply focused on something when that person is talking. I can't have too many stimuli; I need to focus on one thing at a time.

Buffett went to the bridge World Finals in Cambridge. In bridge you must be incredibly focused, working out the probabilities every time you play a hand because you're playing with a partner. You cannot be good at something if you're not working hard. In the same way, you can't focus if you're not working hard. Focus and hard work go hand in hand.

I think it's something never spoken about in all the books I've read, except for one, which is The Snowball: Warren Buffett and the Business of Life. In an interview with Alice Schroeder who wrote the book, she said people don't appreciate how hard Warren works. The reason he's such a good investor, is that he has this database in his head of all the work he's done over the last 80 years. He carries in his head the data of all the investment related work he has done in his life. There are no shortcuts to success, be it in acting or in sport or in investing.

When Jacques Kallis, former South African cricket player would go out to bat in a 5-day test game, and he'd been at the crease facing hundreds of balls, he'd treat each ball as if it was his first ball. – Walter Aylett

Warren Buffett: The Making of an American Capitalist by Roger Lowenstein provides a fascinating insight into the working environment at Berkshire Hathaway and the somewhat recluse behavior of the head honcho.

At Berkshire Hathaway's headquarters, there are roughly 25 employees responsible for dealing with countless Securities and Exchange Commission and other regulatory requirements, filing federal income tax returns, attending to shareholder and media queries, compiling the annual report, preparing for America's biggest annual meeting, coordinating the board's activities and getting Buffett his daily burgers, fries and Cherry Cola.

Buffett believes in a compact organization where his employees manage the business while he focuses on the investment side. He works with masses of data before reaching investment decisions: Buffett calculates the economics as the Company sends him new information. He does not need help from executives to do this.

Clients would send Buffett a package of information. By the time their meeting with him commenced, he would know the notes inside and out. Buffett would calculate the economics on the fly as the client divulged new material. The client often noticed that he had brought no notes with him and had no minions running in and out, prepping him with data. It was all *solo*.

His ability to absorb masses of data and to cut through the clutter suggests a certain genius. His ability to focus intently on his subject and his typically calm demeanor complements his approach at work.

He recognized that adding layers of executives, though each might be bright, earnest, and well-intentioned, would blur his focus. Much of the work they might accomplish would be *unnecessary work*.

One of his "Buffetisms" is that nothing worth doing is not worth doing well. He does not like protracted decision-making or drawn-out and continuous bargaining. His negotiating style is to seek or propose offers on a *take-it-or-leave-it basis*. Once he's decided, he sticks with it. The only person Buffett needed was Gladys Kaiser, his secretary for 25 years. She saw that he wasn't disturbed and answered questions flatly. Because she was fully informed about his business dealings, she knew to keep information confidential, not even sharing it with her husband until it was public knowledge (302).

At work, Buffett keeps to himself. He often lunches alone, sending out for a McDonald's *quarter pounder with cheese and fries*. His managers find him somewhat aloof. He does not organize a schedule in advance, saying people can come any time. In the 90s, Buffett and Bill Scott alone handled the investing, a job divided among scores of traders and analysts at other firms.

Scott was not even employed full-time, and he left the office at three p.m. each day to practice in a polka band. Buffett did the research and made the decisions in sweet solitude, consulting telephonically with his right-hand man, Charlie Munger. In contrast, the Harvard University endowment, the largest academic endowment globally, with roughly the same size portfolio as Berkshire, had a staff of more than 100 (303).

Buffett's co-workers are little more than a backdrop: unobtrusive, robotic, and unerringly dependable. According to his daughter, Susie, "all the people in the office are the same. They don't talk, they just do their work." There's no intellectual peer among his trusty crew. While cheerful with his staff, Buffett is not talkative as he is with his pals. Someone hoping to watch and learn from Buffett would be disappointed. Buffett's daughter noted, "you can't watch it, it's in his head" (302).

If his managers have any complaint about Buffett, it's that he is too far removed. When asked for advice, he's often extremely economical in his answer. He would "drop a pearl", as one of them said – a verse from his Zen of capitalism, intended to shed some light as if his managers, too, were apostles (306).

Unlike the modern CEO, Buffett is known for not blocking out his time in advance, preferring to keep it open. When one of Kay Graham's sons enquired about booking an appointment to see Buffett, he simply said, "Come anytime; I don't have a schedule" (292).

Richard Simmons, President of the Washington Post Company, describes the quiet emerald green inner sanctum of Buffett's office as sparingly outfitted with miniature sculptures of bulls and bears, an antique Edison stock ticker under a glass dome, family pictures, and one of Ben Graham and a dusty, checkered plaid couch. He did not have an electronic calculator, stock terminal, or computer. Buffett was the computer (292).

When Buffett was in his office, nothing seemed to happen except for Scott, Buffett's trader, poking his head in to say, "$10 million at 125, yes or no?"

The phone doesn't ring much, and his days are a veritable stream of unstructured hours and Cherry Colas. He sits at his red wooden desk for hours, connected to the world by telephone, which he answers himself (292).

Buffett often tells the tale about a stranger in a small town wanting to get acquainted with some of the town's folks. The fellow went to the village square and saw an old timer with a mean-looking German Shepherd. Looking at the dog tentatively, he said, "Does your dog bite?"

The old man said, "Nope." So, the stranger started to pet the dog, and the dog practically ripped his sleeve off.

He turned to the old timer and said, "I thought you said your dog doesn't bite!"

The old timer replied, "This ain't my dog." The moral of the story is about asking the right kind of question (297).

According to Buffett, anger drives out rationality. One must apply logic not to fool oneself—the efficiency with which something such as a motor or a business works depends on rationality. One needs intelligence and talent, but these are not enough: habits can creep into one's character and temperament, affecting one's ability to behave rationally.

Buffett's father had often told him to identify the classmate he admired the most by listing the qualities they portrayed. Then he was to list those qualities he did not like in that person. Through this exercise, Buffett identified those qualities which, with practice, he could make his own. He maintains that it is important to ask the right questions for success. At a shared talk on success to the students at Columbia University, he and Bill Gates revealed the secret to what got them to where they are today: rationality.

Focus is perhaps one of Warren Buffett's most noteworthy traits. As a child, he read a book, *One Thousand Ways to Make $1,000*, and according to his biographer, Alice Schroeder, his dream from a young age was to become rich. At the tender age of 11, Buffett set his sights on becoming a millionaire by age 35. As the old truism goes, time will tell. He made his first million by age 30, beating even his own prediction by five years.

One of Buffett's few hobbies is playing bridge, a card game that demands incredible focus. When he's not working or learning, he's busy with bridge, playing 12 hours a week. When asked by CBS News' John Blackstone if there are lessons for business and for later life in the game, Buffett answered, "There's a lotta lessons in it, you must look at all the facts. You must draw inferences from what you've seen, what you've heard. You must discard improper theories about what the hand had as more evidence comes in sometimes. You must be open to a possible change of course if you get new information. You have to work with a partner, particularly on defense."

To describe the extent of his focus, Buffett had this to say to Blackstone. "You know, if I'm playing bridge and a naked woman walks by, I don't ever see her," he said, laughing, then added, "Don't test me on that!" (Crippen, 2008).

Wouldn't it be fun taking you up on that challenge, Mr. Buffett?

· · · · · · · · · · · ·

CHAPTER 8 – RATIONAL THINKING

"You know someone said the chains of habit are too light to be felt until they're too heavy to be broken. And habits really make an enormous difference in your life." – Warren Buffett, Berkshire Hathaway AGM, 2015

In the Spring of 1998, Warren Buffett and Bill Gates came to the University of Washington to share their combined experience and wisdom with college students from the business school. Watching the footage of that meeting, I marveled at how young they were, perched informally on a table on the stage. Buffett was in top form, cracking jokes and looking totally at ease. Before moving on to the open questions, they were asked to talk about what got them to where they are. Buffett said it was not IQ in his case, causing an uproar of laughter from the students. He said everyone in the room had more than enough IQ to perform his job. "The big thing is rationality. I always look at IQ and talent sort of representing the horsepower of the motor, but then in terms of the output, the efficiency of the motor works, depends on rationality because a lot of people start out with 400 horsepower motor and get 100 horsepower of output and it's way better to have a 200 horsepower and get it all into output" (Bill Gates and Warren Buffett || Columbia University, 2017).

Why do some smart people do things that interfere with the 'output' they deserve? Buffett delivered a powerful insight. "It gets into habits, into character, into temperament. It really gets into behaving in a rational manner and not getting in your own way. As I say, everybody here has the ability absolutely to do anything I do and much beyond. Some of you will and some of you won't, but the ones that won't, it will be because you get in your own way, it won't be because the world doesn't allow you to … It will be because you don't allow yourself to" (Bill Gates and Warren Buffett || Columbia University 2017).

He ended with a simple piece of advice that my own father had given me, no doubt picked up from Mr. Buffett! *Apply logic to help avoid fooling yourself. Charlie will not expect anything I say just because I say it, although most of the world will... Never fool yourself, and remember you are the easiest person to fool* – Warren Buffett (Gurpreet, 2018).

My dad would tell me to look around my class and pick the people I admired the most and then write down what qualities I most admired in them. Then, I was to look around at the people I liked the least and write down the qualities about them that turned me off. My lists included qualities ranging from hard work, great sportsmanship, confidence, curiosity, kindness, and even good chatting with girls. I slowly realized that there were certain qualities that, with a little practice, I could make my own. I would attempt to emulate the admired qualities that, Buffett says, become habit-forming with practice. He wisely said that the habits you have in 20 years are the habits you practice today. My dad drummed this into me, and I've tried my best to take this onboard. What drives me is the thought of those dreaded chains when I'm older! Thanks for that, Mr. Buffett.

Aylett & Co is known for integrating rational thinking into their overall business approach. Rational behavior is holistically built into their independent and well-informed investment philosophy. *We are rational, bottom-up in our thinking, looking at assets rather than at the economy,* is a line that I have heard my dad say in numerous meetings.

In an interview at Gibbs Business School, top South African financial journalist Alec Hogg explained Buffett's rationality regarding his investment style.

When doing your work on the intrinsic value of a company, you're buying the company, not the share. Working out intrinsic value is not difficult, Buffett explains. *'Don't try get to the second decimal point, in fact you have a range for your intrinsic value.'* The way he puts it, is that *'if somebody walks through the door, if they weigh 310 pounds or 320 pounds, you don't need to find out their weight to know they are overweight.'*

It's a similar situation with investing. So, you get the intrinsic value, and that rarely changes. That only changes as you get the new financials, and then you're doing your estimate on what you think that company can earn over the next 10 years and work that into your numbers.

Once you have an intrinsic value of a company, you then find what the margin of safety is that you would be comfortable with. So, let's just say the intrinsic value is one Rand, your margin of safety would be 20 percent. So, you don't buy those shares at say 80 cents. And then you let Mr. Market, who is the manic depressive who doesn't have any medication, let him get manic and depressive. But primarily you wait for him to get into one of his depressive phases, so that the share price gets below your margin of safety. That's when you buy, and the period you hold on for is forever. So, there's no trading, there's no punting, there's no watching the share price and saying, 'Oh, that's a good price, that's a bad price.' It's doing your homework (Alec Hogg – Investing the Warren Buffett Way, 2016).

Charlie shared a secret in a video featuring Buffett and Munger's views on reading, uploaded by Infinite Dreams Publishing on YouTube a few years ago.

I have the kind of mind that if I want to read something I can tune everything else out. In fact, I frequently sit in a room and converse with dead people while the people around me are irritated. So, I don't think you should try my methods.

In 'Poor Charlie's Almanack: The Wit and Wisdom of Charles T. Munger', Charlie's reading passion and life hack of reading books written by those passed is evident.

In my whole life, I have known no wise people (over a broad subject matter area) who didn't read all the time—none, zero. You'd be amazed at how much Warren reads—and at how much I read. My children laugh at me. They think I'm a book with a couple of legs sticking out.

I am a biography nut myself. And I think when you're trying to teach the great concepts that work, it helps to tie them into the lives and personalities of the people who developed them. I think you learn economics better if you make Adam Smith your friend. That sounds funny, making friends among the eminent dead, but if you go through life making friends with the eminent dead who had the right ideas, I think it will work better in life and in education. It's way better than just being given the basic concepts.

Okay, so Mr. Munger is encouraging us to learn through reading about those who have gone ahead of us, to find our way, become smarter and improve our decision-making. I guess by reading books by respected people in history who are no longer alive, Munger forges a connection with the works and thinking of these dead authors to benefit his own learning. It sounds perfectly rational and makes one think, doesn't it?

In the Gibbs Business School interview, Alec Hogg explains Charlie's take on learning from others, learning from the mistakes of others, and ultimately improving one's rational thinking.

Charlie has a point. Start reading about these predecessors and it will change your life. So, reading, just learning, just picking up those pools of wisdom from people that you hugely respect because they were so mindful, because they were so clear in their logic, that the clarity of their thought was so different to what we see in this fuzzy world of ours. Through reading and learning, it springboards you on your own journey of exploration and learning. That's what it's been like for me. I've been exposed to people that I never would have bothered with in the past but having taken those first few steps into the world of Warren and Charlie, it's really made such a massive difference in my life. This has had the greatest impact on my life. It's been like having a great teacher who would open doors for you and then you can go explore for yourself.

It got my mind completely focused on what I wanted to do with my life. Part of what they say is to try and do something that you're the best in the world at. On the one hand, invest in yourself and secondly, try and invest in a way that you can become the best in the world, at one thing, at something. You have the chance to be the best in the world in a very small, little area, which is your circle of competence. They talk a lot about this 'circle of competence'. (Alec Hogg – Investing the Warren Buffett Way, 2016).

Ah, 'circle of competence', another of Buffett and Munger's famous secrets of success. That sweet spot of expertise, knowledge, and skill you have mastered, where few can beat you. It's like a smaller circle within a larger circle. Inside the larger circle is what you think you know but aren't totally sure about; inside the smaller circle is what you absolutely do know with a deep certainty—more about this practical and highly effective mental model in the next chapter.

· · · · · · · · · · · · ·

CHAPTER 9 –
CIRCLE OF COMPETENCE

"I'm no genius. I'm smart in spots, and I stay around those spots."
– Tom Watson, Founder of IBM

I have often pondered what sets an extraordinarily successful person apart from all those Joe Average people. Why do 90 percent of people settle into a life of mediocrity? How can one become the Roger Federer of tennis, the Tiger Woods of golf, the Bill Gates of computers, or the Warren Buffett of investments? Yes, these individuals have all worked incredibly hard and are naturally talented, but what really distinguishes their strengths in their fields of competence? How do they maintain their longevity of performance? Take Federer, for instance, still competing at the highest level of tennis beyond his thirties, or Buffett, at 91, still beating industry benchmarks. What is their secret to discovering one's sweet spot?

The answer lies in that small circle from the previous chapter. Take this perfect shape and marry it with your *element*, the thing you are *best* at, and you have your *circle of competence*, the zone where you are *unleashed*. This circular focus creates energy and momentum, allowing your natural genius to grow. In this sweet spot, you can play to your strengths and focus your time and energy on areas that make you soar.

If you're great at only one thing, make it everything. – Roger Federer

From the inception of Aylett & Co in 2005, there has been a Buffett corner in the office, created around the star piece of the Bookworm, a sculptural and sinuous shelving unit designed by innovative Post-Modern designer Ron Arad for Kartell, and bought on a fire sale many years ago by my mother. It houses books written about Buffett and Munger, and alongside are wall hooks decorated with countless lanyards from Berkshire AGMs throughout the years. An array of pictures from the various Aylett & Co pilgrimages to Omaha adorn the wall, along with cartoons of Buffett and Munger. Among the pictures is a diagram of sorts of a baseball player getting ready for a pitch. I always assumed that the player must have been one of Warren or Charlie's favorite players, or perhaps he played for the team they rooted for. The player was Ted Williams, one of the greatest hitters of American League baseball: his team was the Boston Red Sox.

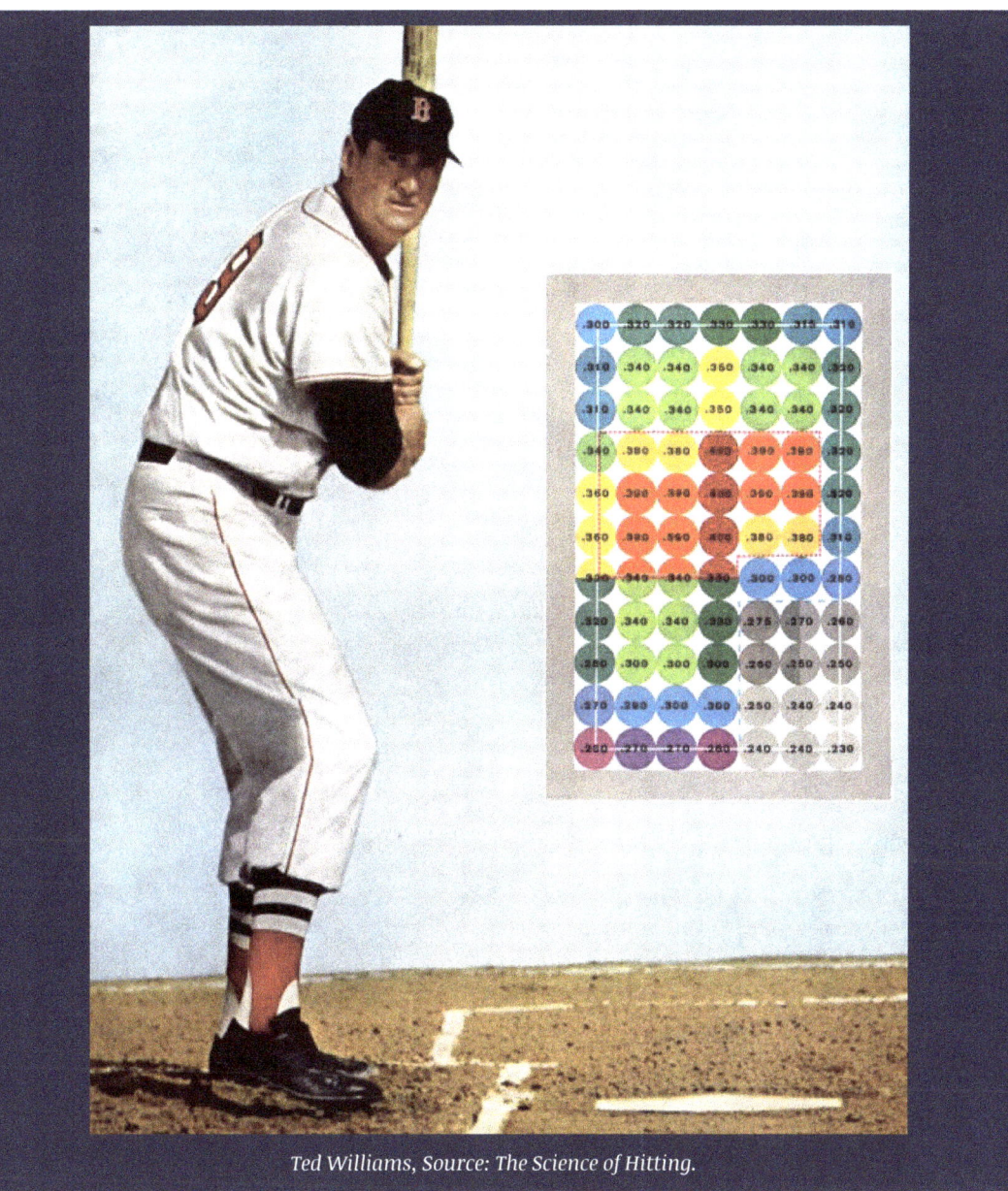

Ted Williams, Source: The Science of Hitting.

In the picture, alongside Ted, is a block showing the strike zone, comprised of 77 circles, each with a number, which determines the circle's color.

The numbers range from .360 to .400. In South Africa, we do not really play baseball and aren't exposed to it much on our sports channels. I figured out that the numbers had something to do with the pitch, but I wasn't sure of their meaning. What's more, what did this picture have to do with Warren or Charlie? It must have meant something because it had a place in the Buffett corner.

The Berkshire Corner at the Aylett & Co. offices. Showered by over 20 years of Berkshire Hathaway AGM lanyards, Berkshire memorabilia, Buffett & Munger books and Ted William's strike zone corner.

Arguably, hitting a baseball is the most difficult feat in sports. Try to catch a peanut in your mouth from someone throwing it at you 100 feet away. This is how Thomas Kaminski, director of athletic training education at the University of Delaware, describes trying to hit a baseball! Why is hitting a baseball so hard? The physics is extreme. In the Major Leagues, the average fastball travels faster than 90 miles per hour. When the hitter faces a ball at that speed from less than 60 feet away, they have 0,15 of a second to react. In the blink of an eye, they must decide whether to hit the ball (Popular Science, 2021).

The average baseball hitter swings and misses a pitch roughly eight times out of ten, which are miserable odds for any sportsman. In 1939, a tall, skinny, frail-looking young man named Ted Williams joined one of the leading American baseball teams, the Boston Red Sox— and resolved to shatter the limits of baseball batting odds by improving his decision-making.

Day in and day out, Williams would practice his swing for hours on end, paying close attention to the "strike zone" where he hit the best balls—Williams' scientific approach to making better decisions as a baseball hitter paid off within a few years. During the 1941 baseball season, Williams achieved a .406 batting average, which means he swung and missed a pitch only six times out of 10. No player since has finished a season with a batting average that high. By the end of his career, Williams had established himself as the greatest hitter in baseball history. He won six batting titles and posted the highest career batting average of any Major League baseball player in the live-ball era, a period that started in 1920 when a series of rule changes was said to make the ball more 'lively' (Wikipedia contributors).

Although the late Ted Williams had a natural baseball talent, he attributed his great success to his rule of "waiting for a good pitch to hit." If he waited for the right pitch in that sweet spot, he would bat at an average of .400.

If he tried to hit pitches in the lower right corner, he would average around .269. Similarly, in an unlikely meeting of minds, nobody embraces Williams' philosophy better than Warren Buffett.

He used the baseball analogy in a Fortune interview in 1974 to explain his investing style. It is unclear whether it was the first time he used it, but the timing was impeccable. Buffett had left his partnership in 1969 at the market peak, only to reappear at the '74 bottom. He relayed a simple message of patience.

I call investing the greatest business in the world because you never have to swing. You stand at the plate; the pitcher throws you General Motors at 47! US Steel at 39! And nobody calls a strike on you. There's no penalty except opportunity lost. All day you wait for the pitch you like, then when the fielders are asleep, you step up and hit it (Interview in Forbes magazine, 1 November 1974).

Ted Williams described in his book, The Science of Hitting, that the most important thing for a hitter is to wait for the right pitch. And that's exactly the philosophy I have about investing— wait for the right pitch and wait for the right deal. And it will come... it's the key to investing.

In investing, I'm in a no-called strike business, which is the best business you can be in. I can look at a thousand different companies and I don't have to be right on every one of them or even 50 of them. So, I can pick the ball I want to hit ...

... Deciding what your game is or where you're going to have an edge is very important. ...

Waiting for a good pitch to hit was the secret to Buffett's most profitable investments, including Coca-Cola, American Express, and Geico (Oshin, 2019).

I slowly started to piece together the connection between Buffett and the baseball picture. Ted had established that the first rule of hitting was identifying a good ball, and he had narrowed it down to percentage points where those good balls were.

The box on the right of Ted represented Williams' "strike zone," with the percentage points broken down into 77 circles, each representing the size of a baseball. The red-colored cells bordered with red dotted lines lay within his "sweet spot". According to Williams, if he waited for a pitch within his sweet spot, he'd hit the ball about 40 percent of the time. But if he grew impatient and swung at pitches just a few inches outside his sweet spot, he'd only hit the ball about 23 percent of the time.

Buffett often refers to Williams' "sweet spot" and draws close parallels to decision-making in investing. *The trick in investing is just to sit there and watch pitch after pitch go by and wait for the one right in your sweet spot. And if people are yelling, 'Swing, you bum!' IGNORE THEM* (Oshin, 2019).

In sports, the area on a bat, a racket, or the head of a club where the ball connects "exquisitely" is called the sweet spot. Having been a keen cricketer and tennis player, I could relate perfectly to what this meant and how it felt when you played a ball off the sweet spot. The best way to describe the feeling is pure bliss. Discovering how to use the "sweet spot" of decision-making to their advantage made Williams and Buffett untouchable. My dad taught this to me as working out your circle of competence and then staying inside that circle.

You don't have to be an expert on every company, or even many. You only must be able to evaluate companies within your circle of competence. The size of that circle is not very important; knowing its boundaries, however, is vital. - Warren Buffett (Yahoo Is Part of the Yahoo Family of Brands, 2017).

Alec Hogg would help in my understanding of how Warren used his Circle of Competence to make smart investment decisions;

When Warren does not understand a company, it doesn't mean he doesn't understand it like I don't understand how to dig a hole for a stadium. He means he does not know where their earnings for the next five years are going to come from, or what they're going to be. His best pal is Bill Gates, who he plays online bridge with every week and Bill is on the Berkshire Hathaway board. The former CEO of Yahoo is also on the board and yet Warren still doesn't buy technology shares.

Buffett tells it, hinting perhaps at his love of Dairy Queen Dilly Bars, a round disk of ice cream on a sucker stick with a delicious chocolate, cherry, butterscotch coating!

When it comes to Microsoft and Intel ... I don't know what that world will look like ten years from now. And I don't want to play in a game where the other guy has an advantage... The software business is not within my circle of competence ... We understand Dilly Bars and not software ... If we have a strength, it is in recognizing when we are operating well within our circle of competence and when we are approaching the perimeter... If you have competence, you pretty much know its boundaries already. To ask the question [of whether you are past the boundary] is to answer it - Warren Buffett (Oshin, 2019).

Anyone for a Dilly Bar?

Charlie agrees with this philosophy, as evidenced by his comment at Berkshire's annual meeting way back in 1999, *Our game is to find a few intelligent things to do. It's not to stay up on every damn thing that's going on in the whole world.* (Berkshire Hathaway AGM, 1999).

Charlie has a simple method to stay within his sweet spot and limit his investment/decision field to sticking to what he knows and understands. There are three baskets for investing, "Yes", "No", and "Too tough to understand."

Circle Of Competence

In today's world, one has unlimited streams of information and opinions at one's fingertips. Through the internet, we have all become 'experts'. My brothers and I often debate 'expertly' with my father, our arguments backed by Instagram stories, TikTok, Wikipedia, social media, Netflix, or Google. On more than one occasion, my dad has dealt with his 'expertly opinionated sons' by reciting a story from *Poor Charlie's Almanack*, of Max Planck, the German physicist who received the Nobel Prize in 1918 and his chauffeur who drove him to the public lectures he gave throughout Germany.

On one occasion, the chauffeur, who knew the lecture by heart by this time, suggested that he and Planck switch places. At the conclusion of the chauffeur's flawless recitation of the lecture, a physicist stood up and posed a very difficult question. The chauffeur, ready for the situation, replied, 'I'm surprised that a citizen of an advanced city like Munich is asking so elementary a question, so I'm going to ask my chauffeur to respond' (Munger, 2006, 66).

In his 2007 address to the University of Southern California Law, Munger clearly defined the distinction between the two types of knowledge.

In this world we have two kinds of knowledge. One is Planck knowledge, the people who really know. They've paid the dues; they have the aptitude. And then we've got chauffeur knowledge. They have learned the talk. They may have a big head of hair, they may have fine temper in the voice, they'll make a hell of an impression. But in the end, all they have is chauffeur knowledge (Parrish, 2015).

How often in life don't you come across people with a 'big head of hair' or who make the loudest noise? In the real world, it is critical to distinguish when you are Max Planck and when you are the 'chauffeur'. If you cannot respond legitimately to this question, you lack true mastery and are probably outside your circle of competence, big hair or not.

CHAPTER 10 – CURVEBALL

2 May 2020

It is 2020. At age 24, I have a finance and marketing undergraduate degree, an Honors degree in strategic brand marketing, and a year of internship beneath my belt. I have time to kill until my student exchange to The Netherlands, which commences in September, and I must feed my creative appetite until then. I approached my father with exciting ideas for Aylett & Co's branding. He smiled across the boardroom table, and he had his own ideas.

He 'curve-balled' my millennial marketing ideas with a somewhat ambiguous proposal.

My boy, I want you to tell a story. I want you to write a book.

Is that so? What does this story entail?

It's a story about how two old men from across the globe who influenced the lives of the Aylett family and influenced Aylett & Company. You millennials are always putting things on your social media stories. Instead, I want you to put some stories on paper and produce a book.

Like most of my father's ideas, there was validity and rationality, but the specifics were scattered, and this year already had various balls in the air for me, including bartending, an online copywriting course, and tennis coaching. Screw it, and let's add another ball.

I immediately suggested joining the upcoming Berkshire trip in May to gather content fueled by the additional allure of some good, old-fashioned American clothes shopping. During my previous AGM trip in 2018, I had been mature enough to scribble notes in a Calvin & Hobbes notebook, but this trip would require a tad more detail. My father happily accepted my initiative. Flight tickets were booked, and hotel rooms were secured. Kimon would officially join Walter and a fellow Aylett & Co analyst at the Berkshire Hathaway AGM 2020. Boy, oh boy, I could taste that Gorat's steak already.

A moleskin notebook in one hand, See's Candies peanut brittle in the other, I would be armed for battle, already anticipating the jetlag after the long haul from South Africa. My eagerness was amplified by the early wake up call to get in line by six a.m. outside the health center. I couldn't wait to breathe in the fresh Omaha air. This would be my third time listening to the two men who unwittingly had a hand in my upbringing. At 16, when I first made the pilgrimage to Omaha, I was an adolescent mess and didn't have the remotest idea of what an honor it was to attend the Berkshire AGM. For my second trip at 22, I wore a formal shirt and glasses to look the part and scribbled notes because it felt like it was the right thing to do, only to stash them away in a drawer back home.

Now at 24, I would be attending with a purpose and sincere appreciation and genuinely cherish this special moment in my life. I would return to South Africa with a book in my mind that would educate, share, and teach worldly wisdom gleaned from these two *'oupas'* (term for grandfather in South Africa) in Omaha, Nebraska.

The 2020 AGM felt special. Maybe it was because the first two digits matched the second two; perhaps it was because I had finally met a nice girl earlier that year. Nonetheless, the shareholders were 'revving'. Warren, 89 and Charlie, 96, were still very much alive and kicking. It felt like sitting and waiting for Federer to serve that first ball of the match against his arch-rivals Nadal or Djokovic. From the fans to the pigeons on the rafters, everyone knew it would be a 'goodie.'

I quickly organized coffee for our group while they went on ahead to bag good seats. While waiting for coffee, I noticed how the crowd had changed since my last visit to see Warren and Charlie. There were fewer suits and more Disney-like fans, all excitedly waiting in queues for the

'Berkshire/Splash Mountain' ride, drenched in Berkshire merchandise.

Chuckling, I knew that by the third hour, they would probably become bored and distracted and amble off to shop for more merchandise, leaving the faithful remaining disciples listening on for several more hours, hanging on to every nugget of wisdom. I rushed to join the group and squeezed into a seat next to my dad.

The lights dimmed, the Coca-Colas were placed by the microphones, and the announcer's voice hushed the crowd. The stage lit up. Here we go.

Instead of Warren and Charlie strolling onto the stage, on walked a Cocker Spaniel accompanied by a Miniature Schnauzer. I felt an iPhone instead of See's peanut brittle in my hand. I was in my bedroom in the family holiday house in Knysna, South Africa, and Warren's voice suddenly filled the room, streaming forth from my iPhone's Yahoo Finance app.

My two dogs hopped onto the bed, cuddled up, and joined me in watching the virtual 2020 Berkshire Hathaway AGM. No 40,000 spectators, no peanut brittle, and to top the Cherry Coke on the COVID cake, no Charlie either.

Mr. COVID had slyly entered the building. He planned to stay and impact everything in his path, from businesses to people, to freedom of movement, to hugging. Imagine the potential romances lost. Overnight it seemed that a global pandemic, supposedly caused by bats in China, had circulated the world. From Cape Town, we still talked over beers about the poor Italians cooped up in their apartments during their lockdown period. A few weeks later, by end of March 2020, South Africa was under lock and key. No socializing, no traveling. Let's not forget the contentious liquor ban.

2020 was to be a steppingstone for me. After juggling a few balls in South Africa, I was set to attend a semester abroad in The Netherlands, go on to do a Masters in Hamburg, and hopefully start a life in Europe. Overnight, the future as we knew it was canceled by an unexpected and severe black swan event that left no country on the globe unaffected. My plans ground to a halt – with no certainty about what lay ahead.

My parents advised my brothers and me to head to our family holiday house in Belvidere, Knysna, for the lockdown period. The three of us had not lived together for some time and certainly not without a parent around. From having our own apartments and living independent lives, it felt as if we had been grounded. On the eve of the first lockdown, there was more than a little anxiety among the Aylett brothers. My middle brother, Nikos, often difficult to tie down, admitted that he was suffering from 'stage fright'. What started as a three-week lockdown slowly progressed to months of brutal restriction, and we and the dogs began looking scruffier and scruffier with hair dressers and dog groomers closed for business.

In 1969, a Swiss-American psychiatrist, Elizabeth Kübler-Ross, wrote in her book, *On Death and Dying*, that grief could be divided into five stages. Likewise, my world was plunged into grief, and mourned for a future lost. At first, there was denial – 'this is surreal, surely it will be over soon, this can't be happening'. This was followed by anger at how a virus from China could affect people worldwide: 'how dare the government close borders, impose a lockdown and set a curfew'? Next came bargaining. If only China had been more responsible, if only there were a vaccination, if only wet markets had been banned.

Depression followed and stealthily set in: how do I proceed from here? My life was then a terrible mess; my future was screwed. 'The world was doomed; we were all going to get the virus; what was the point of anything'? Finally came acceptance and a growing understanding of what the impact of this pandemic meant for me, my family, my country, and our world. At first, I had faith that COVID-19 would have moved on by

May and that our Berkshire trip would go ahead. Alas, the virus showed little sign of loosening its grip.

One lost track of days in the week. It was early May, and I think it might have been a Tuesday. It was hot, and I lazed by the pool, reading a Swedish crime novel. My Cocker Spaniel was circling the property as if he expected a visitor bringing news of sorts. I retreated to the coolness of the kitchen for a peanut butter sandwich. The sound of Mac Miller was floating through the house. An abrupt vibration interrupted the chorus of *blue world*. I peeked at the notification on my screen. Among the various news alerts, a Reuters headline jumped out at me, 'coronavirus forces Warren Buffett to cancel 'Woodstock for Capitalists'. After the World Health Organization had declared the coronavirus outbreak a pandemic, Buffett had no choice but to cancel the live AGM, the largest gathering in corporate America. (Stempel, 2020)

I sat for a while, letting the words sink in - Murphy's law. The year I decided to write a book on Buffett and get the chance to attend the AGM, a worldwide pandemic hit and results in the live AGM being canceled. I guess I was a typical millennial, selfishly bemoaning his problem, ignoring the fact that much graver consequences were affecting the world due to COVID.

I thought back to the analogy of Ted Williams and how he had fundamentally learned, down to percentage points, where those good balls were, those red circles in the strike zone that increased his odds of hitting that perfect, juicy pitch. Leave the bad balls and patiently wait for that perfect pitch.

The millennial generation, born between 1981 and 1996, is known for its demand for instant gratification, fueled by our 'always on' technological environment. We can hardly survive our social media feed taking too long to load, let alone withstand an indefinite delay to our grand plans (Dimock, 2022).

The truth of the matter is that millennials don't like to wait or be held back. COVID literally turned my generation on its head, forcing us to learn about patience in the wake of one of the biggest curveballs of the twenty-first century.

Good old Ted was a master of patience, but as much as I thought deeply about his strike zone model, I was still none the wiser about facing a curveball.

A curveball is a breaking pitch that has more movement than just about any other pitch. It is thrown more slowly and with more overall break than a slider, and it is used to keep hitters off-balance. When executed correctly by a pitcher, a batter expecting a fastball will swing too early and over the top of the curveball ("Curveball (CU) | Glossary").

If followed wisely and patiently, the straightforward bits of timeless advice from Charlie and Warren hold the keys that will let almost anyone, wind up financially comfortable, if not downright rich. Yet while their advice can work wonders, life does have a way of throwing us curve balls. People get fired. Good health is not always a given. Cars get wrecked. Roofs leak. And let's not forget about the COVID-19 elephant in the room. The trick is not to let life's curve balls knock you out.

Allow yourself time to stop and recover, for your thoughts to clear, before making any big decisions. When you feel ready, start making new plans to move forward. Think big, think outside the box, and think differently. Then it's time to implement your plans and follow through, taking baby steps if necessary. I can't help thinking about Charlie, the curveballs he was dealt in the 1950s with his divorce, and the tragic loss of his young son to leukemia. I imagine him taking brave steps to overcome these curveballs and keep moving forward. And here I can also imagine him saying, 'Young man, don't feel sorry for yourself' (Pegler, 2021).

Following Warren and Charlie's advice puts you in a better position to make the right decisions and hit the curve balls when they come flying past. For instance, it's much easier to deal with the costs of a wrecked car if you've got a pile of cash awaiting investment than if you're already in a hole from carrying credit card debt.

While writing this chapter, an article on Aylett & Co was publicized on *Citywire*, a London-based financial publishing and information group. My father was interviewed, and I found one of his answers relevant to the chapter.

The true test of our business was now, in the coronavirus crisis. Nothing changed because there was no pressure on the income statement. We pay low salaries and that model was designed to be able to deal with a shock. As a result, we can make long-term investments. If your income statement is under pressure all the time, you will have short-term thinking. You will run your business, invest, and employ people on a short-term basis. That's not conducive to rational behavior.

We can't always control what happens to us, but we can control how we choose to respond. How we face life's curve balls is an accumulation of past decisions, behavior, and choices. Warren and Charlie are two wonderful examples of well-led lives, enormous wealth and success achieved, and the impact made on others despite having experienced curve balls and setbacks.

A wonderful Japanese proverb was taught to my dad many years ago by his personal trainer, Chris. *Fall down seven times, get up eight*, or in Japanese *Nana korobi ya oki (literally: seven falls, eight getting up)* (Mohamed, 2018).

That's how you face a curve ball.

CHAPTER 11 – GET RICH SLOW

"Compound interest is the eighth wonder of the world. He who understands it earns it; …He who doesn't pays it."
– Albert Einstein

When I told people that I was writing a book that included Warren Buffett in the title, the reactions went along the following lines:

"Interesting, so I assume your book is about how to invest like him and get rich?" or

"Cool! Going to give us tips to become rich like that old guy your father keeps visiting in the States?"

Alas, there is no silver bullet to becoming rich like Buffett. Becoming rich isn't hard; what is hard is the patience it requires. So, for the individuals who have purchased this book to find the holy grail to becoming wealthy like Warren Buffett and Charlie Munger, listen closely: it's actually quite simple.

I am a diehard *Seinfeld* fan. While preparing for this chapter, I listened to the odd episode from the 90s sitcom. I had been working on the content of the 'Get Rich Slow' chapter all day – with no success.

Nothing was jumping out at me. After preparing a fire and going through my family's DVD collection, I picked an episode from Seinfeld Season Four. We took decades to convince my dad to install Wi-Fi in our Knysna holiday home and instead relied on good, old-fashioned DVDs for movies and series.

Seinfeld was embedded in my childhood holiday memories. There was something special about picking out the DVD, inserting it into the DVD player, and picking the episode from the menu tab. Seinfeld was in a class of his own. I admired Jerry Seinfeld as a comedian, writer, and creator. He has influenced my humor and inspired me throughout the years.

Cuddled up with the dogs, I looked forward to the episode. George Costanza appeared in the first scene with exciting news from his public school in Brooklyn.

I got a letter today from the state comptroller's office, you know, when I was going to public school back in Brooklyn. Every week I used to put 50 cents in the Lincoln savings. All right, so, I haven't put anything in it since sixth grade. I completely forgot about it; the state comptroller's office tracks me down. The interest has accumulated to 1900 dollars. They're sending me a check for 1900 dollars! Wow, interest. It's an amazing thing (Seinfeld series, 1989).

Just like that, my writer's block had vanished, like traveling during COVID. *Seinfeld* had saved the day once again, and George had given me the momentum for the 'Money chapter'.

Growing up, my father made me aware that we were in the absolute minority of South Africa's wealth bracket. He would often say, *"We're part of the 1 percent,"* Every new piece of sports equipment, the house we lived in, the overseas trip we went on, my dad and mom would remind us how lucky we were and that our lifestyle was not 'normal'.

As a kid, it was hard to understand that this lifestyle wasn't normal. The friends I had made all attended my private school, which was expensive. Naturally, I benchmarked my life against theirs. Where was this 99 percent that didn't go overseas once a year?

Regardless of whether we had a billion Rand or one Rand to our name, my father would live life the same. He consistently monitored our expenses and watched for bargains. When one was awarded a phone, car, or pocket money, it was calculated to what he thought you *deserved*. My dad would often say that not buying flashy items such as cars could avoid envy and keep one's head below the parapet. *"Keep under the radar, my boy."*

My dad considered buying a Porsche Cayenne, an Audi R8 or a Range Rover at one stage. These car prices in South Africa ranged from 1 million to 2 million Rand then. Aylett & Co had had a corker of a year, and my dad had received one of his highest bonuses to date. I was interning at Aylett & Co then, and on a rainy Tuesday night, I clocked off work and decided to visit him. My younger brother had mentioned that Dad had fetched his new car earlier that day. Excited for the big reveal, I patiently waited for the driveway gate to open slowly. *Surely, he went for the Range Rover… hmm, maybe he manned up and opted for a Mercedes G-Wagon.*

There in the driveway stood his brand-new car: a plain white Volkswagen Golf. I drove a similar model and was perplexed at his decision to downgrade from his previous BMW Coupé to a Golf. A Golf? My dad simply explained. *This car costs me 1/8 of the price of the others. Now I can spend the rest on traveling around Greece.*

I will never forget the sight of that car in my dad's driveway nor the Buffett-like grin etched on his face. He and I once arrived at a supper function, and most of the other guests had arrived in luxury vehicles parked in front of the venue in the 1 million Rand plus bracket. We neatly parked next to a Mercedes G-Wagon. At the dinner table, the questions ranged from, *Is that your holiday car?* Or *Is that a rental?*

Someone that night asked me how I generate content for my book and if I ever hit writer's block. I smiled and replied; *The content is all around me. Daily I stumble upon ideas for the chapters.*

Buffet would go on countless trips to New York. He would ring up friends from his hotel, usually The Plaza, and say, *Could you bring over a six-pack of Coca-Colas? You can't believe what room service charges!* Meanwhile, Buffett was collecting six-figure checks. When Warren was asked how it felt to be a millionaire, he simply replied, *I can have anything I want that money will buy; but I always could* (Lowenstein, 1995:86).

Regarding the game of investing, Benjamin Graham, Warren Buffett, Charlie Munger and Walter Aylett all vouch that investing doesn't require genius and needs reasonable intelligence, sound principles and, most importantly, character quality.

Price is what you pay, value is what you get - Benjamin Graham

If I was offered the chance to go into a business where people would measure me against benchmarks, force me to be fully invested, crawl around looking over my shoulder, etc., I would hate it. I would regard it as putting me into shackles (Charlie Munger, 2006:101).

The secret is to have one's own standards. Aylett & Co is steadfast in making investment appraisals independent of the market. In the world of investing, it is key to watch prices, not current events. Long-term investors are not buying because the price is increasing today or next month; they're buying because the company will be a good business ten years from now, regardless of current events. Don't buy or sell based on news headlines. Maintain a strong balance sheet and cash on hand so that you're never forced to sell for the sake of cash.

This is perhaps a hard lesson learned by the amateur investors who proliferated during the pandemic using DIY apps like Robinhood that made it easy for novices to trade cheaply via their mobile phones. The S&P 500 rose spectacularly since the app launched in 2012, and inexperienced investors piled in lured by rising markets and the deceptive ease of making money investing in meme stocks and cryptocurrencies.

It's been a long 14 years since the last bear market in 2008. Stocks started declining in 2022, and the difference between luck and skill showed up for many first time investors, shutting down the party. The rising cost of living and higher interest rates have had Robinhood customers running for the hills amidst losses and the specter of a bear market. Perhaps reasonable intelligence, sound principles, and a healthy dose of patience are emerging as the true heroes of investing.

In investing, just as in baseball, to put runs on the scoreboard, one must watch the playing field, not the scoreboard - Warren Buffett.

My father often refers to Warren Buffett when discussing how he runs his investment company. Buffett treats stocks as businesses he takes a stake in because they are well-run, and he understands what they do. He sees their long-term earnings potential, choosing quality businesses priced at fair value. One of a medieval castle's most important features was its moat for defense. Warren Buffet has been referring to his moat analogy for decades. To be successful, a business must have a definite moat, also known as a competitive advantage, which allows it to maintain pricing power and better-than-average profit margins.

What we're trying to do, is we're trying to find a business with a wide and long-lasting moat around it, protecting a terrific economic castle with an honest lord in charge of the castle (Wenning, 2021).

What we're trying to find is a business that, for one reason or another – it can be because it's the low-cost producer in some area, it can be because it has a natural franchise because of surface capabilities, it could be because of its position in the consumer's mind, it can be because of a technological advantage, or any kind of reason at all, that it has this moat around it. But we are trying to figure out - why is that castle still standing? And what's going to keep it standing or cause it not to be standing 5, 10, 20 years from now? What are the key factors? And how permanent are they? How much do they depend on the genius of the lord in the castle?
- Warren Buffett (Investment Masters Class, 2022).

The word "debt" in the Aylett household was considered a spell from the Dark Ages. You stayed away from it. My father would drum it into our heads, *Stay away from debt. Debt will kill you, or rather go to bed supperless than rise in debt.*

He consistently showed us examples of how individuals had fallen into the treacherous debt trap.

I would come home from a friend's house, excitedly tell my dad about their fancy house and expensive cars, and ask him how this family became so rich.

How do you know this family is rich, my boy?

Come on, Dad, they have several fancy cars, their house is gigantic and modern, and all the kids have the latest phones.

Well, my boy, you must ask yourself how this family paid for these luxury possessions. Do they have personal debt, a credit card, or mortgage bonds? Most importantly, do they have money in the bank, cash, or an umbrella for a rainy day?

I was unsure exactly how I would find this out, but I got my dad's debt drift, nonetheless.

It's a very sad thing. You can have somebody whose aggregate performance is terrific. But if they have a weakness, maybe it's with alcohol. Maybe it's being susceptible to taking a little easy money. It's the weak link that snaps you frequently in the financial markets, and the weak link is often borrowed money. Debt is the financial temptress, the fatal weak link. - Walter Aylett.

Personal finance is not the sexiest topic, but if only more people mastered their personal finances, they'd wise up to how sexy their lives could be. I am dumbfounded why personal finance isn't a compulsory part of the school and university curriculum. People, even smart ones, can be unbelievably dumb when it comes to rationally managing their money. The steps and principles followed in successfully managing one's money are not rocket science; the younger one starts, the better your chances are of becoming rich. A good start is to set money goals, both short-term and long-term goals. Short-term goals fall into the five-year plan, such as sticking to a budget, creating an emergency fund, starting to invest, saving up for a holiday, and paying off debt. Long-term goals may cover things like early retirement, paying off a mortgage, and having multiple income streams. After setting money goals, creating a budget is the superhero of personal finance. It may sound draconian, but how do you even start to manage your money monthly without a budget? Today this is even easier with so many free budgeting apps that help you track your personal finances to show what you're earning versus what you're spending and what needs to be tweaked. Pay off high-interest debt and save for retirement.

For young people, saving for retirement may sound silly. It isn't, and you can't start early enough. My brothers and I are all in our twenties and have already started investing in retirement annuities. If you don't save for retirement, plan to work in your retirement. It's that simple. How you save for retirement is super important, and here it's back to Warren and Charlie. Invest long-term, invest rationally with a good margin of safety, and stick to sound principles. This isn't to say that you must self-invest; for many, this will be outside your circle of competence. Do your homework when choosing an investment manager or financial adviser, and stay informed!

Lastly, borrow as little as possible.

My partner Charlie says there are only three ways a smart person can go broke: liquor, ladies and leverage, he said. Now the truth is — the first two he just added because they started with L — it's leverage - Warren Buffett (Kim, 2018).

When teaching young people about financial management. I would ask the question: who's the best financial accountant? And you get all kinds of answers. The truth is, the old-fashioned housewife used to be given her monthly allowance of, say, 1000 Rand cash per month, and it would go into a drawer. And from that drawer, she had to pay for food, clothes, extras, and all kinds of household expenses.

And she always followed principles which today they do in companies. In other words, she would always buy stock just in time, like food. She didn't buy it when it would go off; she would buy it when she got the right prices. She would buy volume. In other words, get discounts.

She bought quality at a great price. As the month went on, and she could see she was running out of money, she would hold back because she had seen that there were another five days left. So, she didn't spend the money; somehow, she always had a plan B. In case the milk went off, she had powdered milk. She always had contingency plans.

She never went under. So, she would always have money left over to pass on to the next money and be able to buy herself a frock when the money came in. So principles like stock management in a company, buying at the best prices, not borrowing money on credit cards, and not paying high interest rates. She did everything with a cash flow basis operation, so money was in the drawer. She lived from that, she would start holding back when she was running low on cash, never going into an overdraft. So, in my mind, she's the best accountant. - Walter Aylett.

My dad learned valuable lessons about business when as an articled clerk, he helped his father with the books for his gas station.

One of my most important experiences was when my father owned a gas station and car workshop. I worked as an article clerk and would help my father do his books. It became apparent to me how a business really operates, the economics of the business. In my opinion, it was a very tough business that he ran.

When analyzing the books, we would typically move from the fuel sales to the workshop revenue. What turned out to be a goldmine was the convenience store that sold fast food, sweets, cool drinks, bread, milk, and so on. The convenience store had been added to the business and was run by my mother. That experience set the scene for me to become a successful investor.

Suddenly I was not only an analyst but a business manager; later in life, I heard Buffett talk about being a good investment manager by understanding inherently what makes for a great business.

Being involved in my father's business taught me about cash flow, and I have taken that lesson throughout my career right to this day. I focus on cash flow. What's the payback? What's rational? If I can't understand it, I'm not interested. The experience of working in that small business environment was extremely helpful. Interestingly enough, Buffett worked in his grandfather's store, although I suspect I had it easier helping in my father's business. At least there was no snow to shovel!

From the age of about twelve to the time I left home, I used to read voraciously. My father and I read all the time. We had no television, only the radio and books. My dad would bring home the National Geographic, and I would go to the book exchange and the library and bring home books on war and history, and even comic books like Tintin and Asterix & Obelix. My father and I just devoured these books. I always asked myself, when will I ever use this information?

Throughout my entire life, I have read. Even when I studied and when I was working, I carried on reading. Through reading, my mind expanded from history to geography, all the way across subjects that included esoteric writings by authors like Deepak Chopra. This was another of the lessons I learned from Charlie Munger and Warren Buffett; the importance of reading.

I've no doubt I would not have been as successful today had I not gone through the experience of constant reading, having a passion for finding undiscovered wines, and working in a small family-owned business, getting an understanding of how true businesses work. This had nothing to do with investing but with understanding business. The two-year military service, compulsory in South Africa when I was young, gave me discipline and taught me to toughen up and grow up. Careerwise, I gained investment experience, but I never forgot the most important common sense principle. I wasn't a very clever guy, but what helped was that I knew what I could do and what I couldn't do.

"So, Walter, what's the one-liner to getting rich?"

"Spend less than what you earn, stay away from debt, and have patience."

· · · · · · · · · · · · ·

CHAPTER 12 – TAP DANCING TO WORK

"You ought to be happy where you are working. I always worry about people who say, 'I'm going to do this for ten years, I don't really like it much, but then I'll do ten more years there'". **That's a little like saving sex up for your old age, not a very good idea.**
- Warren Buffett

This career advice by Mr. Buffett has often been quoted, and I guess another way of saying the same thing is for people to seize the day for life is, after all, finite.

Do something you love so that you can wake up in the morning and tap dance to work. My father borrowed this line from Warren; I must have heard it a thousand times. It may take time and much soul-searching to work out what you love doing and what feeds your passion. I was almost 24 before I worked out that I love creating content and was able to tease out a strategy that would allow me to follow that path. Since my teenage years, I had firmly believed that I wanted to follow in my dad's footsteps and work at Aylett & Co in the field of investments.

During my postgraduate degree in strategic brand marketing, I also interned at my dad's company rotating from the back office, to marketing, to the investment team. I experienced incredible personal conflict and turmoil during that time, unwittingly realizing that the investment world wasn't for me.

I came alive creating content, developing copy for brand strategy, and drawing inspiration from the worlds of fashion, travel, music, art, and culture and creative icons like Banksy, Sam Kolder, Roy Lichtenstein, Andy Warhol, and the street artist, Alec Monopoly. I finally worked out that I wanted to be a strategic creative.

In 2012, during my visit to the Berkshire Hathaway AGM, I got the chance to visit Warren Buffett's home in Omaha. I couldn't go in to look around but could view it from the driveway leading directly off the street.

There was no 6-foot wall, no electric fencing, just a simple set of poles linked with a chain to deter people from walking right up to the front door. I was around sixteen then and knew a bit about Warren but little about his somewhat quirky and unusual lifestyle. I was excited when we joined the crowds in Farnam Street, waiting to sneak a peek into the home of one of the richest men in the world. I was with Justin, a newly recruited investment analyst at Aylett & Co.

When he and I had maneuvered our way to the front, I saw the opposite of the Buffett home I had envisioned. The man with a net worth of over $89 billion lived in a house that seemed more suitable for a modest retirement complex. Instead of the luxurious, impressive mansion befitting an enormously wealthy person, there stood a simple family home, neat as a pin and almost proudly reflecting a deep modesty. Alec Hogg, who is from South Africa, describes the Buffett home as an ordinary house that you would find in maybe an upmarket suburb of Johannesburg.

I would later find out that the house had been bought in 1958 as a family home for the princely sum of $31,500. This house seemed downright frugal for one of the world's richest men, valued at .001 percent of his total net worth. I stood there in the driveway and truly felt lost for words. This was so at odds with my generation's nouveau riche influencers and celebrities, propped up by luxury brands, flaunting their success and wealth.

• • • • • • • • • • • •

Justin Ritchie and I standing outside Mr. Buffett's house in 2012. And no, we did not mean to color coordinate for the occasion.

This man, Warren Buffett, could have any house in the entire world, yet he chose to reside in the simple Nebraskan home he had lived in for decades. He clearly liked consistency: driving the same Cadillac for a decade and ordering one of only three McDonald's breakfasts, on his short drive to the office, depending on the stock market's performance that day – if he felt flush, it would be the slightly more expensive bacon, cheese, and egg biscuit, if the market was down it would be the cheaper two sausage patties. Clearly, it's not a question of affordability. I think Mr. Buffett enjoys playing this game with himself, a morning ritual that signals the state of the markets for him!

His office space is no different from his home. It struck me that the man likes continuity. Buffett has lived in the same house since 1958 and has been based in the same office building for more than 50 years. He employs 25 people in the small Berkshire Hathaway headquarters in Omaha, Nebraska.

Going back throughout Berkshire's existence, you'll find the same 25 individuals. They don't change. Warren had a formula – simple and effective. My 16-year-old head was spinning on the way back to the hotel, *The man hardly seemed to spend any money, but he was always smiling! What's the big secret?*

I knew Charlie's method (avoid the things that make you unhappy to be happy). Now I was curious to know Warren's secret. Later that night, my father, Justin, and I dined at another example of Warren's consistent lifestyle habits, Gorat's Steakhouse, where he's been a regular customer for decades.

We decided to order Warren's regular: a T-bone steak with a double side of hashbrowns and a Cherry Coke.

The other famous activity to do when visiting Omaha was to visit Gorat's Steakhouse, which is one of Warren's favorite dining spots. Again, in a

South African context, it's nowhere near what you would find in a grill house, but it's an Omaha steakhouse, and you go where Mr. Buffett goes, and you ask for what Mr. Buffett eats, and you end off with the double chocolate sundae, even if you never do have dessert because that's what he does. And it's that kind of experience you get just to try one day, to walk in Buffett's shoes. – Alec Hogg.

With a life-size cardboard cut-out of Warren Buffett joining us at our meal, I decided that this was the perfect time and place to ask my dad the question that had been worrying me the entire day.

What makes Warren so goddamn happy? If it's not extravagant, materialistic possessions, it could be drinking Cherry Coke, watching Nebraskan football games, or playing bridge on weekends. What's the catch here, Dad?

My dad was in his element, teaching Buffetology to his son while sitting in Warren Buffett's favorite steakhouse. The environment undoubtedly made this particular Buffett chat with my dad extra special and memorable.

My boy, I can start off by saying that one thing's for sure: old Warren wakes up every morning and tap-dances to work. He loves his job, and he loves the people he works with. The money isn't what drives him. It's the game of investing. Achieving the eighth wonder of the world, compound interest. He's a lifelong learning machine. That is why at the tender age of 87, he can still be as alive as, dare I say it, more alive than the younger Warren was.

Charlie often praises Warren for getting better and better as he gets older. He's not slowing down. Warren and Charlie are both amazing examples of people who don't stop working; they haven't retired. As they've moved into their 80s and 90s, nothing has changed. They've kept working, and it seems they are well on their way to working until age 100.

Warren jokingly maintains that he will retire five years after he dies, giving the Berkshire Hathaway directors instructions via an Ouija board. He probably wasn't joking, either, and I think that's just the kind of thing that would amuse Warren.

To be a lifelong learning machine, one must constantly acquire fresh knowledge and insight. Today, information is more readily available than ever before. Online courses and content are at our fingertips and free to access via the world wide web. Recently, I did an online masterclass in short storytelling with Neil Gaiman, the English author. One aspect he focuses on is how one draws inspiration from many influences.

For instance, as a tennis player, I draw inspiration for my game from Warren Buffett's investment thinking; *if it's close to the line, it's out*. Investing and tennis are two completely different worlds, yet I've learned from one and applied learning to the other. By consistently learning, one's mind stays nimble and agile, and I am convinced this is key to Buffett's and Munger's longevity.

All these influences go onto your personal 'compost heap' of inspiration. Gaiman thinks ideas result from the confluence of two things coming together. My dad further enlightened me about being happy, again inspired by Buffett:

Now, my boy, the key to happiness with the type of job or career you choose is to go out in the world and look for the job you would take if you didn't need the money. You really want to think about what will make you feel good when you get older about your life, and you at least generally want to keep going in that direction.

Ralph Rigby, a textile salesman, visited Omaha and found Buffett in a state of ecstasy. *A lot of guys studied baseball stats or the Racing Form, Buffett on the other hand, merely had a hobby that made him money and that was relaxation to him* (Lowenstein, 1995:164).

We had now ordered a couple of beers, and my dad was on a roll, in full Buffett mode. Word for word, I recognized the Buffett one-liners.

The next key to being happy is having your own standards. That way, you can never feel as if you've disappointed someone or let your teacher down. It suddenly does not become, 'Am I going to scrape a pass for this module?' but rather, 'Is it going to be an 80 percent or a 90 percent?'

I just knew that Charlie's wisdom would come into play sooner or later. I was right.

And remember what Charlie said, my boy. Spend each day trying to be a little wiser than you were when you woke up.

Perhaps one of my dad's all time favorite inspirations from Charlie is: *If you read each night before you head to bed, you'll wake up smarter the next day.*

I've always known my dad to be a voracious reader across various genres. He believes that to be a smart investor; one must love constant reading on the topic.

Discharge your duties faithfully and well. Step by step, you get ahead, but not necessarily in fast spurts. But you build discipline by preparing for fast spurts.

Eventually, the conversation moved to include quotes from Poor Charlie's Almanack: *Instead of living with high expectations and worrying about what will come next, follow Munger and slug it out one inch at a time, day by day, and at the end of the day — if you live long enough — like most people, you will get out of life what you deserve* (Munger, 2006:138).

I cannot tell you how often my father would say, *Under-promise, over-deliver my boy; that way, you'll never disappoint*. I wanted to know from my dad how these guys make all this money, hardly spend it, and still stay happy.

My boy, the real treasure in keeping happy is not the money, and it can help sometimes, but the real secret, according to Buffett, is being surrounded by the right values and with the love of friends and family.

Charlie agrees that close friends and family are very important. He told author Janet Howe for her book *Damn Right! Behind the Scenes with Berkshire Hathaway Billionaire Charlie Munger*; While no real money came down, my family gave me a good education and a marvelous example of how people should behave, and in the end, which was more valuable than money (Lowe, 2003:21).

My dad continued, cracking open his third beer. *And what's more, my boy, always take the high road…it's less crowded.*

Munger had often said that by taking the "high road" in business, he decided to be transparent and ethical in what he sells to people instead of selling stuff that tricks them. *I would choose that approach even if I made less money, but in fact, I think you make more. You've got a huge advantage on the high road. There aren't too many competitors* (cnbc.com).

My dad's seminar on 'the secret to happiness' concluded with a rather cheeky comment from the waitress who had been eavesdropping on our conversation about her famous weekly customer.

I'll add one more thing to your dad's answer… for goodness sake, my dear, you're young and full of future life experiences. If there's one thing you take from old Warren Buffett: Don't save sex for when you're 80!

The table erupted with laughter!

I could swear that Warren's cardboard cut-out winked at me at that exact moment.

My dad and I with fellow Aylett & Co analysts Corné Van Zyl and Alex Philippou, 2018. Eating at Buffett's usual weekly lunch spot, Gorat's Steakhouse, where he's been a regular customer for decades.

THE END

BERKSHIRE 2023

Exhausted after a long Berkshire day, my dad's words, "Let's go, my boy," were a welcome relief. The Berkshire Annual General Meeting of 2023 was nearly at a close. We had endured waking up at five a.m., waiting in the AGM line for a good few hours, and listening to Warren and Charlie's words of wisdom for most of the day while battling jet lag from our flights. As we hurriedly gathered our Berkshire goodies and approached the exit, I suddenly halted, gripping my dad's arm urgently. Anxious, I asked if we should take one last look, just in case.

Confused and exhausted, my dad asked, "Just in case of what?" It was clear he, too, was eager to leave. Disheartened, I explained, "Just in case Warren and Charlie aren't here next year." Despite his reluctance, I insisted that we return for a lingering gaze of the two Berkshire Gramps.

Turning back, we positioned ourselves by one of the entrance stairs, absorbing the sight that had become so familiar over the past few decades. A panoramic stadium filled with 40,000 attendees worldwide, listening intently as two old men shared their personal and business wisdom. Warren, at 92 years old, and Charlie, at 99, were the epitome of experience. As I focused on the spotlights illuminating Warren and Charlie's podium, I strained to hear Charlie's grumbling voice amidst deep thoughts of this 'moment's awareness'. But my attention was captivated by the visual spectacle before me.

Combating my fear of Warren and Charlie's hourglass running out were two playful signs placed before Warren and Charlie: "AVAILABLE FOR SALE" for Warren and "HELD-TO-MATURITY" for Charlie. There were also clips from past meetings in the Berkshire movie featuring questions about Berkshire's succession plan. Warren and Charlie were clearly sending a message. It reminded me of Roger Federer's last ten years in tennis, consistently asked about retirement yet continuing to excel. Similarly, Warren and Charlie continued to play and win 'grand slams.'

My dad began to walk away, signaling our departure. Taking a deep breath, I followed suit. The last thing I caught was Charlie's response to a question about artificial intelligence. "I'm personally skeptical of some of the hype that has gone into artificial intelligence; I think old-fashioned intelligence works pretty well."

Farewell, Charlie. See you at your century.

Kimon and Walter at the Berkshire Hathaway AGM 2023.

AFTERWORD

This book took over three years to complete. I began the overall process before the start of the COVID-19 pandemic. It has been one of the most challenging projects that I have encountered. The actual writing of the book was the fun part. The editing and proofing were where the nightmares started. I want to thank my editing 'team.' Individually you all did your part.

- Jackie Aylett
- Brenda and Hugo from Busy Bee Editing
- Veronica Bowker
- Jonathan Amid
- Helen Aylett

My mother, Jackie, played a crucial role in the editing process. She spent many hours 'operating' on the patient. I also have to pay tribute to inheriting her gene of having a strong grasp of the English language, most likely passed on by her mother, Veronica Bowker. Jackie also initiated my first-ever Berkshire trip in 2012 and has since then fueled many exciting ideas that developed the process and execution of this book.

I would also like to thank Phillipa Mitchell for guiding me through the treacherous self-publishing process. Gregg Davies for layout expertise. Tammy Manson for illustrating my visions for the creation of the book. Lara Wellner for the cover.

Thank you, Sasha, for helping me get through this crazy time between my personal life, running my business, and getting this book out there. You are a gem of the earth and deserve love.

Lastly, for my father, Walter.

Thank you for taking me to Berkshire and sharing Warren and Charlie's worldly wisdom.

- Afterword -

Their insight into life has helped me and has shaped my overall thinking. Their wisdom is so simple yet extremely hard to execute practically. It helps to see my dad apply those principles to his life, family, and Aylett & Co Fund Managers.

I sincerely wish that this book can extend the privilege I've been fortunate to experience in learning from the wisdom of Warren and Charlie.

My dad reading one of his Christmas presents in our haven house, Knysna 2005.

- About the Author -

ABOUT THE AUTHOR

Kimon is 27 years old, living in Cape Town, South Africa. He wrote this book at age 24. It all started in February 2020 when Kimon approached his father, Walter, with marketing ideas for Aylett & Company Fund Managers. Instead, Walter came up with an idea for Kimon to write a book based on the story of two men in Omaha, Nebraska and how profoundly they had affected a man, his family and his investment company, thousands of miles away in South Africa.

By March 2020, Covid had started shutting down the world. The lock down environment was the perfect setting to write a book.

Kimon has inherited traits from both his mother and father and is creative and analytical. From a young age, he held a strong command of English and excelled in creative writing and public speaking.

He joined his father, Walter Aylett, at the 2012, 2018, 2022 and 2023 Berkshire Hathaway Annual General Meetings. In 2024, he will make his fifth long trek to Omaha, Nebraska.

He assists Aylett & Company Fund Managers with brand management, strategic content, and overall marketing. He has a deep passion for the family business.

Kimon founded a content creation agency in 2020, Blackswan & Co Digital. Alongside his involvement at Aylett & Company Fund Managers, he maintains a strong interest in creating content under the Black Swan brand.

Kimon is an avid tennis player, traveller and loves all things Greek. When in Cape Town, he is more often than not accompanied by his Cocker Spaniel, Gus.

REFERENCES

Nelson Mandela Foundation. Db.nelsonmandela.org,/speeches/pub_view.asp?pg=itemItemID=NMS135txtstr=ChrisHani. Accessed 30 July 2020.

Becoming Warren Buffett. HBO Documentary Directed by Peter W. Kunhardt, produced by Teddy Kunhardt & George Kunhardt. 2017.

Kaufman, Peter, et al. Poor Charlie's Almanack: The Wit and Wisdom of Charles T. Munger, Expanded Third Edition. 3rd ed., Walsworth Publishing Company, 2005.

Lowe, Janet. Damn Right: Behind the Scenes with Berkshire Hathaway Billionaire Charlie Munger. New edition, Wiley, 2003.

Lowenstein, Roger. Buffett: The Making of an American Capitalist. Illustrated, Orion Publishing Co, 1997.

Charlie Munger: "Every Mischance in Life Was an Opportunity to Learn Something." | USC 2007 [Ep.172]. www.youtube.com, www.youtube.com/watch?v=FZoxaDuM8Ag. Accessed 30 July 2022.

Warren Buffett's Opening Statement at Salomon Brothers Testimony – the Talkative Man. www.talkativeman.com/warren_buffett_salomon_brothers_testimony/. Accessed 30 July 2020]. "Buffett and Munger a Wealth of Wisdom." YouTube, uploaded by Buffett and Munger a Wealth of Wisdom, two Mar. 2022, www.youtube.com/watch?v=4VZcP1ic8ho.

Miles, Robert. The Warren Buffett CEO: Secrets from the Berkshire Hathaway Managers. Wiley, 2003.

Schroeder, Alice. The Snowball: Warren Buffett and the Business of Life. Updated & Condensed ed., Bantam, 2009.

Elkins, Kathleen. "Warren Buffett Says the Most Important Decision You'll Ever Make Has Nothing to Do with Your Money or Career." CNBC, 14 May 2018, www.cnbc.com/2018/05/14/warren-buffett-says-the-most-important-decision-is-who-you-marry.html

Daniel Sloss. Performer. JIGSAW, 2018, Netflix, www.netflix.com.

Schwantes, Marcel. "Warren Buffett Looks for Intelligence and Initiative When Hiring People. But Without This Third Trait, 'the First Two Will Kill You.'" Inc.Com, 6 Feb.

- References -

2020, www.inc.com/marcel-schwantes/warren-buffett-says-you-should-hire-people-with-3-traits-but-only-1-separates-successful-people-from-everyone-else.html.\ https://medium.com/@iantang/3-kinds-of-friends-you-meet-in-life-6b03c8383a85.

Wikipedia contributors. "Pilgrimage." Wikipedia, 19 July 2022, A pilgrimage is a journey, after which the pilgrim returns to their daily life.

Robert Miles - Warren Buffett Biographer Part One." YouTube, 2 Sept. 2008, www.youtube.com/watch?v=fsivP-fek54.

Hiddleston, Tom. "Bill Gates: 'I Didn't Even Want to Meet Warren Buffett' —but Their First Dinner Conversation Changed Everything." CNBC, 11 Dec. 2020, www.cnbc.com/2019/11/08/bill- gates-i-didnt-even-want-to-meet-warren-buffett.html.

Katharine Graham | Biography, The Washington Post, and Facts. Encyclopedia Britannica, 13 July 2022, www.britannica.com/biography/Katharine-Graham.

"Thank You, Warren, for Your Generosity." Bill & Melinda Gates Foundation, www.gatesfoundation.org/ideas/articles/warren-buffett-philanthropy. Accessed 23 Aug. 2022.

Crippen, Alex. "Warren Buffett: Playing Bridge Theoretically More Interesting Than Naked Woman." CNBC, 2 Apr. 2014, www.cnbc.com/2008/02/19/warren-buffett-playing-bridge- theoretically-more-interesting-than-naked-woman.html.

"Bill Gates and Warren Buffett || Columbia University 2017 ||." YouTube, uploaded by Columbia Talk, 14 June 2017, www.youtube.com/watch?v=6G7RDwFrOG0.

Saluja, Gurpreet. "Legends on Independent Thinking." Gurpreet Saluja Financial Services, 15 Nov. 2018, www.gurpreetsaluja.com/legends-on-independent-thinking.

"Alec Hogg - Investing the Warren Buffett Way." YouTube, 4 Apr. 2016, www.youtube.com/watch?v=L4ApYgc_xsY.

"Hitting a Baseball Is the Hardest Skill to Pull off in Sports. Here's Why." 26 Apr. 2021, Popular Science, www.popsci.com/story/science/why-is-hitting-a-baseball-so-hard.

Svoboda, Martin. "History: I Call Investing the Greatest Business in the World ... | Quotes of Famous People." Quotepark.com, quotepark.com/quotes/1926088/history. Accessed 27 Oct. 2022.

Oshin, Mayo. "Warren Buffett and Ted Williams on How to Make Better Decisions in Life and Work." Ladders | Business News & Career Advice, 11 Oct. 2019, www.theladders.com/career-advice/warren-buffett-and-ted-williams-on-how-to-make-better-decisions-in-life-and-work.

Wikipedia contributors. "Live-ball Era." Wikipedia, 30 Sept. 2022, https://en.wikipedia.org/wiki/Live-ball_era.

Parrish, Shane. "The 2 Types of Knowledge You Should Know About." Time, 15 Oct. 2015, time.com/4070788/planck-chauffeur-knowledge.

Hathaway, Berkshire. "Afternoon Session - 1999 Meeting." CNBC, 2 Nov. 2018, buffett.cnbc.com/video/1999/05/03/afternoon-session-1999-berkshire-hathaway-annual-meeting.html.

Yahoo Is Part of the Yahoo Family of Brands
finance.yahoo.com/news/warren-buffett-simplifies-trick-investing-191754258.html. Accessed 27 Oct. 2022.

Warren Buffett Quote: Investing, just as in Baseball, to Put Runs on the Scoreboard, One Must Watch the Playing Field, Not the Scoreboard. quotefancy.com/quote/931026/Warren-Buffett-In- investing-just-as-in-baseball-to-put-runs-on-the-scoreboard-one-must. Accessed 28 Oct. 2022.

Wenning, Todd. "Pay Attention to the Castles Behind the Moats." Intrinsic Investing, 24 June 2021, intrinsicinvesting.com/2021/03/17/a-moat-without-a-castle.

"Moats." Investment Masters Class, mastersinvest.com/moats. Accessed 28 Oct. 2022.

Kim, Tae. "Buffett, Quoting Partner Munger, Says There Are Three Ways to Go Broke: 'liquor, Ladies and Leverage.'" CNBC, 26 Feb. 2018, www.cnbc.com/2018/02/26/buffett-says-out-of-the- three-ways-to-go-broke-liquor-ladies-and-leverage-leverage-is-the-worst.html.

"Roger Federer." TIME.com, 19 Apr. 2018, time.com/collection-post/5217613/roger-federer.

Mills, Rhiannon. "Queen Elizabeth II - a 'Selfless' Monarch Who Made Britain Proud." Sky News, 8 Sept. 2022, news.sky.com/story/queen-elizabeth-ii-a-selfless-monarch-who-made-britain-proud-12692845.

Stempel, Jonathan. Capitalists."Coronavirus Forces Warren Buffett to Cancel 'Woodstock for 13 March 2020, https://www.reuters.com/article/us-health-coronavirus-berkshire-idUSKBN2101SA.

Dimock, Michael. "Defining Generations: Where Millennials End and Generation Z Begins."

Research Center, 21 Apr. 2022, www.pewresearch.org/fact-tank/2019/01/17/where-millennials- end-and-generation-z-begins.

- References -

"Curveball (CU) | Glossary." MLB.com, www.mlb.com/glossary/pitch-types/curveball. Accessed 28 Oct. 2022.

Pegler, Lindy. "How to Cope When Life Throws You a Curveball - Ascent Publication." Medium, 12 Dec. 2021, medium.com/the-ascent/how-to-cope-when-life-throws-you-a-curveball-61b97adf688b

Mohamed, Arthir. Fall Down Seven Times Get Up Eight, 4 December 2018, www. https://www.linkedin.com/pulse/fall-down-seven-times-get-up-eight-mohamed-arthir/.

• • • • • • • • • • • •

www.ingramcontent.com/pod-product-compliance
Lightning Source LLC
Chambersburg PA
CBHW062047290426

44109CB00027B/2755